DECKS

DECKS

The Editors of Creative Homeowner Press

CREATIVE HOMEOWNER PRESS®

Manufactured in United States of America

Current printing (last digit)
10 9 8 7 6

Produced by Roundtable Press, Inc.

Project editor: William Broecker
Contributing editor: Don Nelson
Assistant editors: Marguerite Ross, Philip Reynolds
Photo research: Martha Richheimer
Illustrations: Norman Nuding
Design: Jeffrey Fitschen
Jacket design: Jerry Demoney

LC: 89-091776
ISBN: 0-932944-89-2 (paper)
        0-932944-90-6 (hardcover)

CREATIVE HOMEOWNER PRESS® BOOK SERIES
A DIVISION OF FEDERAL MARKETING CORP.
24 PARK WAY, UPPER SADDLE RIVER, NJ 07458

Acknowledgments/Photography Credits
*The editors of Creative Homeowner Press would like to thank the following individuals and
companies for their assistance in preparing this publication:*

California Redwood Association
405 Enfrente Drive, Suite 200; Novato, CA 94949
14 (James Woodhead, designer/owner), 16 (Jain Moon & Scott Foell, designers), 49 (John
Hemingway, designer), 54 (Woodhead), 55 (Elsebert Jegstrup, designer), 60, 65, 73 bottom right
(John Matthias, designer), 118 (Russ Slater, designer), 121, 138 (Eddie Assa/Ace Custom Decks,
Inc., builder), 139

Cording Landscape Design, Inc.
Franklin Turnpike; Ramsey, NJ 07446
Len DiTomaso, ASLA
52, 53, 134, 135, 136, 137

Georgia-Pacific Corporation
900 SW Fifth Avenue; Portland, OR 97204
56, 58, 59

Mr. and Mrs. Joseph Laurite
124–125

Louisiana-Pacific Corporation
111 SW Fifth Avenue; Portland, OR 97204
5, 9

LSL Associates, Inc.
Route 45; Pomona, NY 10970
Stuart Leventhal
78, 79, 115

Dr. and Mrs. Kalman Post
12

Secor Farms
168 Airmont Avenue; Mahwah, NJ 07430
66, 72

Southern Forest Products Association
Box 52468; New Orleans, LA 70152
64 top

The Spa Shop
213 Route 206 North; Flanders, NJ 07836
Karl Schoenwalder
13, 69, 74, 114 bottom, 116, 117

Stockpile, Inc.
52 Maltbie Avenue; Suffern, NY 10901

Mr. Bruce Weber
113

Western Red Cedar Lumber Association
Yeon Building; 522 SW Fifth Avenue; Portland, OR 97204
2, 114 top

*Creative Homeowner Press would also like to thank the following photographers for allowing us to
use their photos in this publication:*

Glen Allison: 61, 123

Mark Becker: 118

Hedrich Blessing: 80

Michael Bliss: 144

Ernest Braun: 16, 49 top, 55, 60, 65

Karen Bussolini: 73 top, 122 (Nelson Denny, designer)

Paul Cleveland: 64 bottom

Jerry Demoney, photographer, and Ann Demoney, stylist for Stockpile, Inc.: 12, 13, 52, 53, 66, 68,
69, 70, 71, 72, 74, 76, 77, 78, 79, 113, 114 bottom, 115, 116, 117, 119, 124, 125, 128 bottom, 130, 131,
132, 133, 134, 135, 136, 137, 140, 141

Barbara Engh: 73 bottom right

Phillip H. Ennis: 120, 127 bottom (Stuart Narofsky, architect)

John Fulker: 114 top

Lynn Karlin: 75

Michael Landis: 10, 11 (Russell Ireland, designer), 15 (Ireland), 50 (Dave Woosey, designer), 51,
57, 65

Peter Loppacher: 121, 138, 139

George Lyons: 14, 54

Peter Mauss/ESTO: 62, 63

Norman McGrath: 67 (Mark Simon of Centerbrook, architect), 126 (Kroeger & Perfido, architects)

Kent Oppenheimer: 142, 143

Robert Perron: 73 bottom (Robert Mueller, designer), 127 top (Mueller), 128 top (Mueller), 129

Tom Rider: 49 bottom

Randy Shelton: 5, 9

Cover photograph courtesy California Redwood Association: Ernest Braun, photographer; Eli
Sutton with HBM, architect.

*Creative Homeowner Press also gratefully acknowledges the editorial contributions of
Kent Keegan, Pamela Keegan, Dennis Getto, and Eric Brubaker.*

Introduction

Every year, thousands of homeowners are getting more from their outdoor space. That's because they're creating *more* space and beautifying their homes at the same time with a new deck. Now, with *Decks*, you'll find that today's decks give you more ways to enhance the value of your home than ever before. You'll find ideas and methods for custom-designing a deck to suit your personal style. And, if you have some basic carpentry skills and the right tools, you'll find illustrated, step-by-step instructions for building your own dream deck.

Safety First

Though the designs and methods in this book have all been safety-tested, it is not possible to overstate the importance of using the safest construction methods possible. What follows are reminders; some do's and dont's of basic carpentry. They are no substitute for your own common sense.

• *Always* be sure that you've got a safe electrical setup; be sure that no circuit is overloaded, and there is no danger of short-circuiting, especially in wet locations.

• *Always* read the labels on containers of paint, solvent, and other chemical products; observe ventilation, and all other warnings.

• *Always* read the tool manufacturer's instructions for using the tool, especially the warnings.

• *Always* use holders or pushers to work pieces shorter than 3 inches on a jointer. Avoid working short pieces if you can.

• *Always* remove the key from any drill chuck (portable or press) before starting up.

• *Always* pay deliberate attention to how a tool works so that you can avoid being injured.

• *Always* know the limitations of your tools. Don't try to force them to do what they weren't designed to do.

• *Always* make sure that any adjustment is locked before proceeding. For example, always check the rip fence on a table saw or the bevel adjustment on a portable saw before starting to work.

• *Always* prevent the workpiece from spinning on a drill. It will tend to spin clockwise, the same as the drill rotation. Clamp and block the piece whenever necessary.

• *Always* wear a mask and rubber gloves when sanding or handling chemicals.

• *Always* wear a respirator mask when cutting pressure-treated wood with a power saw.

• *Always* wear eye protection, especially when striking metal on metal; a chip can fly off—for example, when hammering a chisel.

• *Always* be aware that there is never time for your body's reflexes to save you from injury from a power tool in a dangerous situation; everything happens too fast. *Be alert!*

• *Always* keep your hands away from the business ends of blades, cutters, and bits.

• *Always* try to hold a portable saw with both hands so that you will know where your hands are.

• *Always* use a drill with an auxiliary handle to control the torque when large size bits are involved.

• *Always* check your local building codes when planning new deck construction. The codes are intended to protect public safety and should be observed to the letter.

• *Always* hire a licensed electrician to install outdoor lighting for your deck.

• *Always* hire a competent building contractor to construct a deck raised more than 6 or 8 feet off the ground, or built on an unstable or steeply sloping ground.

• *Always* install railings for any deck standing more than 24 inches above grade and for all stairs and ramps. Follow local building codes for proper height, number of wood members, and materials.

• *Never* work with power tools when you're tired or under the influence of alcohol or drugs.

• *Never* work with very small pieces of stock. Whenever possible, cut small pieces off larger pieces.

• *Never* change a blade or a bit unless the power cord is unplugged. Don't depend on the switch alone being off; you might accidentally hit it.

• *Never* work in insufficient light.

• *Never* work with loose clothing, hanging hair, open cuffs, or jewelry.

• *Never* work with dull tools. Have them sharpened, or learn how to do it yourself.

• *Never* use a power tool on a workpiece that is not firmly supported or clamped.

• *Never* saw a workpiece that spans a large distance between horses without close support on either side of the kerf; the piece can bend, closing the kerf and jamming the blade, causing saw kickback.

• *Never* support a workpiece with your leg or other part of your body if you intend to cut it with a portable or jig saw.

• *Never* carry sharp or pointed tools, such as utility knives, awls, or chisels in your pocket. If you want to carry tools, use a special-purpose tool belt with leather pockets and holders.

Contents

This handsome deck and hot tub installation has several unusual design features. The split level tub enclosure has flanking steps and a wall for privacy. The angled design of the platforms complements the octagonal shape of the tub. The broad-capped railing steps down to echo each change of level.

Broad one-step levels lead to an octagonal corner area that commands the choicest view. It is just right for two or three people to gather. The skillful use of simple, well-proportioned elements in the railing is clearly visible on the stairs to a lower level.

Broad-plank decking, low wood walls, and planters lead to a private area in this garden. The open-frame roof can support climbing vines.

A raised deck continues the flow of interior space out into the open air and around the building. The roof unites the inside and the outside while providing shade and protection from the weather.

Activity areas on this low, completely open garden deck are defined by the placement of easily moved furniture. A single full-width step provides unrestricted access from the patio.

Woods and a stream-fed swimming pool make up the beautiful view seen from this deck. The dramatic angled outline at the pool's edge is a notable feature.

A moderately raised deck connects the house with a stone barbecue; broad steps continue on to
the yard and gardens.

(Opposite) The decking around this house surrounds a handsomely constructed hot tub in a secluded corner.

(Below) This striking home is surrounded with broad, low decks that lead to social areas and a swimming pool.

Activities can be separate, or can flow together across the long continuous steps that join the two levels of this deck. The low wall and plantings provide privacy and wind protection to the pool area.

1 A DESIGN CHECKLIST

A deck makes an inviting extension of your indoor living space—it becomes an outdoor room. Before you start constructing a deck, make a thorough investigation of the factors that influence the design and planning of a deck. There are some important questions you need to consider. What do you want your deck to do for you? How do you and your family intend to use your deck? How is the deck going to function with the existing site?

The design of a wood deck—large or small—should be determined before any construction begins.

FUNCTIONAL CONSIDERATIONS

By answering the question "What do I want my deck to do for me?" you identify the ideas that will lead to a successful design solution. Ask yourself whether you want a very formal outdoor area primarily for entertaining large groups of people, an outdoor area only for family use, or simply a space for informally entertaining small groups of people. Will you use the deck for sunbathing or as the location of a swimming pool? Will handicapped or elderly people be using the deck? Must the deck be completely secure from the outside? Is privacy important?

When you have answered these questions and considered those given below, and after you have carefully evaluated your life-style, you can more intelligently choose the wood deck design that will best suit your needs.

AN ATTACHED DECK

A deck that is attached directly to a dwelling becomes an extension of the interior living space; a covered deck makes the connection even more pronounced.

A FREE-STANDING DECK

A deck that stands apart from a house creates new living space outdoors. It may focus recreational activities around a pool or a hot tub, as shown here.

ANSWERS FOR PRACTICAL QUESTIONS

How are my present living spaces used? In answering this question, keep in mind that a deck is often best located near a kitchen area or family room. Another popular deck location is near or adjacent to the dining room. The deck should be situated near the heaviest traffic flow in the house, and it should be built in an area that can be easily modified without drastically changing the normal operation of the household. Keep in mind that the closer the deck is to your kitchen, the fewer steps you'll have to take carrying food and beverages back and forth. If you prefer a small, private deck, consider building one off a bedroom or bathroom.

How large a deck do I need? There is no standard answer to this question, since individual needs vary greatly. But you should provide about 20 square feet for each person using the deck—a comfortable but not excessive space. This converts to an area 4 feet by 5 feet, which provides room for a chair and space to circulate. If you regularly entertain groups of 15 to 25 people, for example, you will need 500 square feet, which is an area about 20 feet by 25 feet or the equivalent. Remember that there are limits to what a reasonably sized deck can hold. If you contemplate having groups larger than 15 to 25 people, the deck should be situated to take advantage of your site, so that the overflow can be handled without overcrowding. If the immediate area around your deck can be used by larger groups, you might find that a smaller deck will function far more efficiently than a grandiose one. Be realistic about your space needs. Often a clever arrangement of furniture or plants can give the impression of a much larger space and yet preserve the charm of a more intimate area.

Your choice of a ground-level or an elevated deck will be determined partly by the configuration of your site and by access to the deck from your house and the site. A deck situated on a second-floor level is often the only alternative available on a steeply sloping site. A deck at ground level, however, can provide a larger surface, which might be required to accommodate

AN ATTACHED, LOW-LEVEL DECK

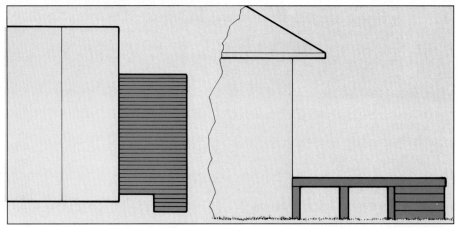

The simplest deck to design and construct is built close to the ground, and is directly accessible from the ground floor of the house and from the surrounding yard. Plan view left, elevation right.

A FREE-STANDING DECK WITH STAIRS

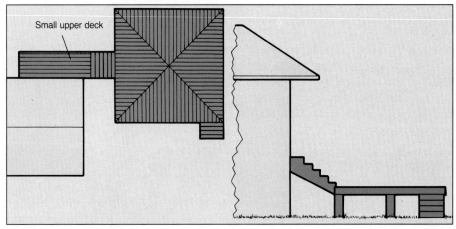

Small upper deck

A more complicated design places the deck free of support from the house to create a more independent space. Stairs lead up to a small deck (hidden in elevation view) attached to a second story.

A RAISED DECK ON A SLOPING SITE

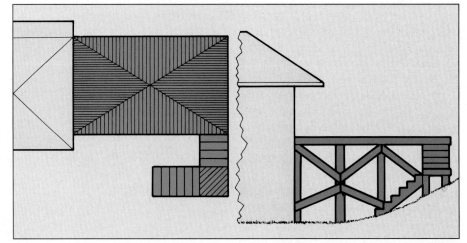

Building a deck at a higher level above a sloping site requires particular concern for proper post foundations, as well as bracing for the extended posts.

your particular needs and your site. It also offers a wider choice of construction materials.

How will I use the deck? Decide first whether you need a formal or informal area. A deck subjected to continual wear and tear from children and pets must be sturdy as well as suitable for adult needs. An informal arrangement, constructed of relatively heavy-duty materials and incorporating built-in furniture, is often the best choice for such a deck. It requires less attention to details and gives more layout options.

A formal deck is usually less subject to hard, constant use, and so it would be appropriate to consider lighter-weight materials, movable outdoor furniture, and decorative details such as trellises and flowerbox borders.

Do I want privacy? The openness of a deck depends on how much privacy you want. While there are other considerations that affect the degree of openness (see Site Considerations, page 21, and Climatic Considerations, pages 23–25), the need for privacy often dictates the final design solution. Keep in mind that there are three types of privacy: visual, acoustical, and physical.

Defining each of these three types is important because you may be concerned with one, two, or all three. Each requires a specific architectural treatment. Special considerations for each type of privacy are explained below.

Visual privacy. Ask yourself: Is protection from being seen, or from seeing others, necessary? You may discover that the most desirable exposure for your deck faces an unsightly yard, street, or railroad tracks—not to mention the houses or apartments nearby that look into your outdoor space. To correct these conditions and gain visual privacy, here are some recommendations.

A simple wood fence (see Chapter 9) high enough to screen out the undesirable view or low brick or decorative concrete block walls used in conjunction with vertical shrubs can create an effective screen. Rows of shrubs of varying height can limit the view into and out of your space. A lattice covered with ivy or similar creeping vines is another effective screening technique. If

HEDGES AND SHRUBS FOR PRIVACY

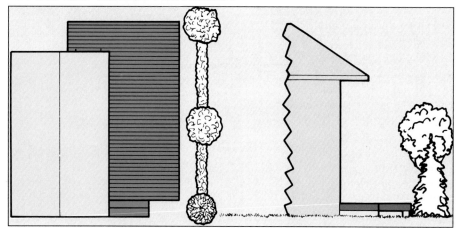

The simplest way to create visual privacy for a deck is to plant shrubs, bushes, and hedges to screen the deck from neighbors and streets. This preserves the outdoor character of the deck.

SOLID WALLS FOR PRIVACY

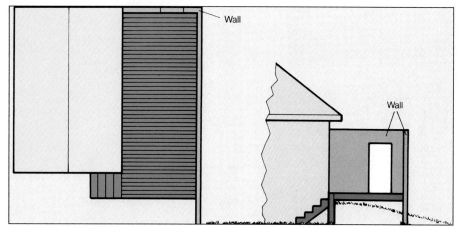

If your deck plans demand visual privacy and security, solid walls are an obvious solution. They tend, however, to limit the outdoor character of the space.

A TREE-TOP DECK FOR VISUAL PRIVACY

To obtain complete privacy, as well as security, build your deck up in the tree tops, attached to the second story. This creates an independent space inaccessible to intruders. Deck and railing are not attached directly to trees, to allow for wind.

you want overhead screening for your deck, then consider building a trellis roof structure in combination with ivy or other vines. But keep in mind that this might reduce the overall light level. Another option is to build a wood framework to support a roof of translucent plastic or fiberglass panels. This guarantees a high level of privacy from above but doesn't block sunlight.

Acoustical privacy. Do you need protection from unwanted or bothersome noises? While no method is perfect, acoustical isolation—using readily available materials and landscaping—in most instances can offer sufficient protection from distracting noises. One method that is attractive and effective uses plantings of shrubs or evergreens. For example, evergreens placed across the path of the noise source will break up the noise so that it will merge with background noises. A fence, in combination with vertical evergreens or shrubs, gives additional isolation from noise sources that are exceptionally severe. An urban or suburban lot will require more privacy than an isolated country site. Since it is impossible to stop all noise from penetrating your outdoor area, keep in mind that an exterior deck is by its nature open. The more you enclose your deck, the more likely it is that it will lose flexibility and desirability. You must balance your needs.

Physical privacy. This includes protection from intrusion by unwanted guests or pets, and can also be thought of as security. While fences with controlled access or lockable gates prevent strangers from wandering in off the streets, low walls with evergreen shrubs may provide all the physical privacy you need. To accurately evaluate your needs, you must answer the following questions: Do you want to control access to your deck? What kind of security do you want or need? This will depend in part on whether or not the deck is enclosed in any manner. Do you need a method of keeping youngsters out of or inside the area? Are there mandatory requirements for fences in your area? For example, a swimming pool next to your deck must be enclosed in a secure fence of a certain minimum height.

A ROW OF SHRUBS FOR ACOUSTICAL PRIVACY

A dense wall of shrubbery will cut down noise from the street or from neighbors quite effectively, without seeming to enclose the deck space.

A LATTICE FENCE FOR PHYSICAL PRIVACY

A wooden fence of open design denies access to the deck, creates visual privacy, yet allows prevailing breezes to provide ventilation.

A MASONRY WALL FOR SECURITY

For the utmost in physical privacy and security, surround your deck with a masonry wall; it will also provide acoustical privacy.

SITE CONSIDERATIONS

When you have clearly identified what functions you want your deck to fulfill, the next step is to understand the physical and environmental limitations of your site. These restrictions have as much influence over the physical design of your deck as your functional requirements. It is essential that you evaluate the following considerations.

Terrain. The location of your deck and the type of structure you choose may be dictated by the terrain. A flat area with firm, stable soil will require a minimum of support. If the terrain pitches either toward or away from the house, then posts, footings, and bracing will have to be more elaborate. The slope of the terrain in relation to your house is very important in determining the design and structure of your deck.

Utilities. Before starting any deck construction, it is essential to determine the location of all utility lines, both underground and aboveground. Water, gas, sewer, and telephone lines running under your intended deck area will influence your planning. Special construction may be necessary, or either the lines or the deck may have to be relocated. Accidents can easily occur as a result of not knowing where and at what depth the lines are located.

To locate these lines, check with the customer service departments of your local utility companies. They will help you determine the precise location of their service installations on your property. They may also suggest ways of building over or around the problem. If your house was built recently, your local building inspector will probably have a copy of your utility, gas, water, and sewer hookup locations. Keep this information in your files for future reference. It may be that no connections or underground lines exist under or near the proposed deck site. Most often, utility lines are located in a zone from 2½ to 8 feet below ground level. Normally, the major concern is that the location of deep footings will conflict with the utility service.

You can see the path of any aboveground, overhead utility lines, such as telephone or electric wires. You probably will not want to locate a deck directly beneath them, especially if you

plan to construct a roof structure.

Codes. Building codes are intended to protect public safety. The building codes in force today are very specific. Although local requirements may vary, most building codes stipulate that all exterior decks not in direct contact with the ground must be able to support at least 60 pounds per square foot. While this figure may appear excessive, it takes into account the effect of snow loads in northern climates as well as the effect of a large group of people standing on the deck. All design recommendations and sizes found in this book have been calculated to meet that loading requirement. Building codes also stipulate that second-story railings on the exterior of the house must be either 36 inches or 42 inches high to keep the area safely contained.

Before construction begins, you must obtain a building permit from your local building inspector's office. This office may require one or more sets of your plans (see Chapter 3 on how to draw a plan). When reviewing your plan, the inspector will make sure that

your proposed design and construction meet all applicable codes.

Zoning. Zoning laws control land use and the density of building in prescribed areas. They specify setback requirements, which state how close you can build to any property line, the height of fences and trellises, and in some cases, what materials may be used. They may specify how much of your lot may be covered by structures.

If your plans conflict with regulations, you can apply for a variance, that is, a permit to build a structure that does not conform in detail to the law. Your local building department can explain the procedure. There may be a public hearing at which neighbors' opinions are considered. There is usually a fee. Be sure not to put up a structure that violates your local zoning laws and codes. A building inspector's report could lead to a legal order to tear it down.

Determine whether there are any easements located on your property. An easement is a right-of-way granted to a utility company or other property owner that is spelled out in your prop-

A SITE SKETCH FOR DECK PLANNING

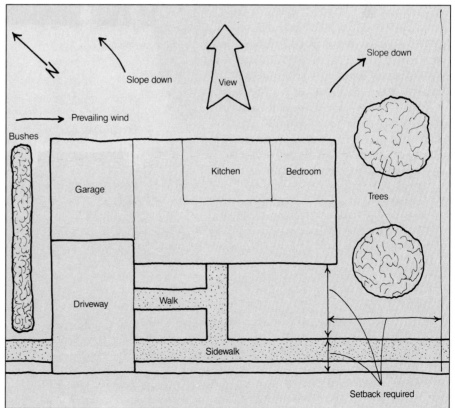

As the first step in getting your design ideas on paper, make a scale drawing of your existing site, including trees and plantings, property lines, and the prevailing winds.

erty deed. It must not be blocked or restricted. Your deed may include other stipulations that limit the design or even the location of a new structure. Check your deed before you build.

Soil conditions. Even if soil conditions around your house are normally stable, remember that minor excavation should be filled in as soon as possible to reduce settlement of surrounding soil into the excavation. Soils with a high clay content tend to swell during the spring; this can cause movement of the deck. Get professional help to solve difficult soil problems. Most other types of soil are considered quite stable for deck support.

Plants and trees. In planning an outdoor space, take inventory of the existing plants and trees in the construction area. Evaluate the relative condition and the survival ability of each plant or tree before you decide to move it to another location. (Your local nursery or grower can advise you about the hardiness of any particular plant or tree.) Remember that a minimum of transplanting and cutting is the most satisfactory course; this reduces your total replacement costs. To move a mature tree that is located where you want a deck is impractical, and cutting the tree down is not a good solution. Instead, design the deck to include the tree by leaving an opening around the trunk.

Once you have chosen a deck location, make a sketch of the area and mark those plants or trees that can be kept and those that must be moved.

Pools. If you are planning a pool as part of your deck design, locate the closest water supply source. It is important to minimize the length of run of pipe required to service the pool. In northern climates, make sure that the water pipe can be pitched from a high to a low level so it can be drained. Your pool contractor can advise you on safety restrictions on pool access.

Electrical needs. Lines to supply deck electrical outlets and lighting must be planned well in advance of construction. The need for an underground cable from your main service panel or the possibility of through-the-wall connection should be considered when planning the location of the deck.

STRUCTURAL CODE REQUIREMENTS

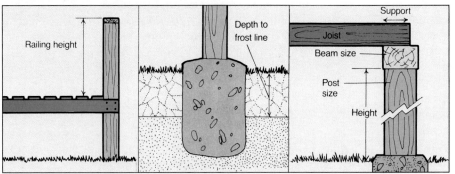

Local building codes may specify what railing heights you must use, how far below the frost line post foundations must go, as well as the sizes of the wood structural members of your deck.

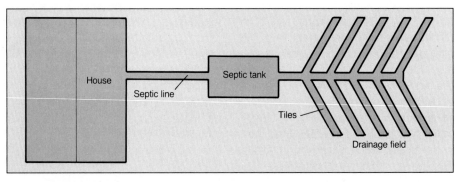

Before deciding where any holes are to be dug or any structures built, be sure to locate all the parts of your septic system, so that you can avoid interfering with them.

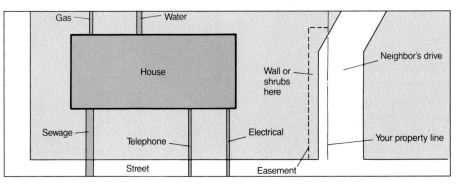

On the site sketch mark the locations of all utility lines, especially those that are buried, as well as property lines and easements that may have been granted to neighbors.

SITE CODE REQUIREMENTS

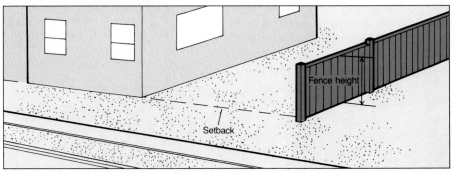

Local codes may restrict the locations and dimensions of fences and other structures in relation to the street or to next door neighbors.

CLIMATIC CONSIDERATIONS

Environmental and physical factors that affect the amount and type of light, the volume and direction of wind, and the control of rain and snowfall all have a profound influence on your deck design. An exterior location chosen solely for the view it provides might be unusable when these factors are taken into account. The following specific considerations will assist you in understanding the basics of environmental design.

Orientation. The first step is deciding what direction your outdoor space will face. This will affect the amount of sun and shade the deck will receive.

A north-facing space in the northern hemisphere will be in shade most of the day. While this is the most desirable exposure in a southern climate, it could be cold and uncomfortable in the north. In a southern climate, the next best orientation is an easterly exposure, so that morning sun falls on the deck.

In colder or more severe climates, a southwest exposure provides full afternoon and late afternoon sun. This will make your outdoor space usable as long as possible and keep it warmer on many cool spring and fall days.

The activities you are planning for the deck can influence its orientation. Sunlight may or may not be a desirable factor, whatever the climate. You must evaluate your needs regarding the quality and quantity of light. North sky light is far more diffused than direct sunlight. That difference will influence your plans for the level of sunlight.

The position of the sun in the sky and the angle of the sun should also be considered. The angle of the sun is higher during the summer months than the winter months. This means that in the winter a south-oriented deck will receive less direct sunlight than during the summer. If you are considering a fence or other obstacle on the southern side of your deck, keep in mind that it may block a considerable amount of the low-angle sunlight during the winter. However, sunlight will fall across most of the outdoor area during the summer. Especially in southern regions, overhead trellises or lanais are used to control the amount of direct sun. In northern climates they may provide too much shade.

SUMMER SUN AND SHADE

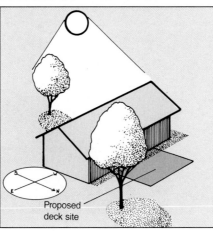

In the northern hemisphere, the noonday summer sun stands high in the sky; buildings and trees cast little shadow.

The late afternoon summer sun is as far to the north as it will go; there will be minimal shade on the north and east of buildings.

SPRING AND AUTUMN SUN AND SHADE

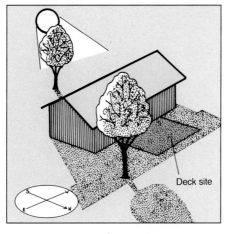

The noonday sun in spring and autumn is partway to its zenith; buildings cast considerable shadows, as do fully-leafed trees.

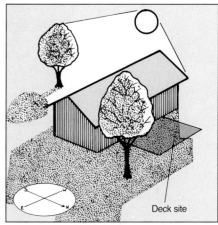

The late afternoon spring and autumn sun is fairly low in the sky; there is much shadow on the north and east sides of buildings.

WINTER SUN AND SHADE

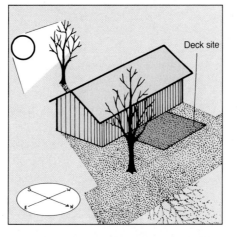

The winter sun is at its lowest point; buildings cast the deepest north-side shadows of the year; leafless trees cast none at all.

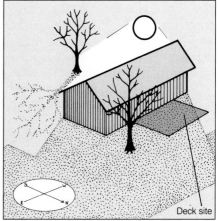

The afternoon winter sun stands low and to the south; buildings cast very deep shadows to the north and east sides.

Wind. If your site has a breeze during the entire day, some form of windbreak is called for. Planning to accommodate the wind's movements means observing the wind pattern around your house. Recall where the leaves collect in the fall; this might indicate a zone of little air movement.

In southern climates, air movement is a definite advantage. Air moving under a shade device feels cooler than a breeze in direct sunlight. A sunshade can help to cool the interior of the house. The cooling effect will be more noticeable from a sunshade located on the windward side of the house. Evaluate the location of your deck in terms of daytime breezes and night air movement. If you are fortunate enough to have a consistent wind pattern, position the deck to take advantage of it. Breezes are easily directed and controlled by appropriate placement of screens, fences, or hedges. In zones where air movement is minimal, locate the deck so that air will be funneled through the deck structure.

Rain. Rainfall on a deck can have pleasing or damaging consequences. Rain falling on a deck makes patterns and movements that can be aesthetically pleasing to ear and eye, but if the deck is not pitched to shed water, ponding or puddling can result. Rainfall is particularly detrimental to your house if the roof is pitched toward the deck. In some cases minor flooding can occur, especially if the deck is on the same level as the house. This is why it is wise to make the deck level a few inches lower than the adjoining interior floor level. Keep in mind that all horizontal exterior surfaces should be pitched away from the house no less than 1/8 inch per foot. If the floor boards—called decking—will run parallel to the house, with 1/4-inch spaces between, slope is not critical. But if the decking will run perpendicular (with the ends at the house side), will be laid without spacing, or will be covered with exterior-grade carpeting, then the deck must slope away from the house 1/4 inch per foot. Be sure adjacent areas can handle rain runoff from the deck.

Snow. The effects of snow and rain are similar in the weathering of a deck. All materials tend to decay under the

TYPES OF DECK VENTILATION

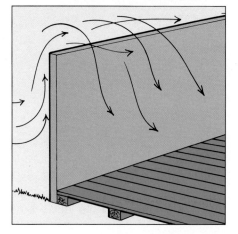

A solid wall deflects most breezes over the deck, while allowing gentle ventilation near the wall.

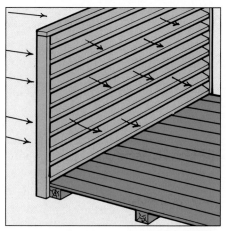

A louvered wall lets all air currents through to the deck; slanting the louvers up or down can direct the breezes as you desire.

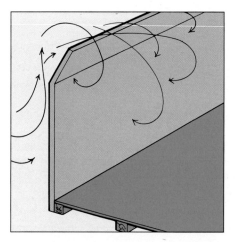

A solid wall with an inward-angled extension draws air currents down, creating movement near the wall.

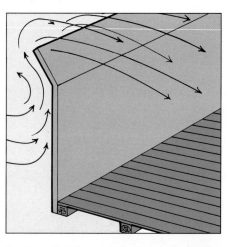

A solid wall with an outward-angled extension deflects air currents up and over the deck, creating a still area near the wall.

Panels in a glass-walled deck can be hinged to permit any desired degree of ventilation by prevailing winds.

Shrubbery and trees will deflect and moderate prevailing winds, allowing some gentle ventilation of deck areas.

influence of weathering. Thus the appearance of all of the materials you use to construct your deck will change naturally over the years. Each material has its own patina of weathering. A well-selected group of materials may look incompatible during construction, but will blend together in a most pleasing manner after a period of exposure to wind and rain and snow. Look for examples of weathered materials that you like on decks that are a few years old. Make your selection of materials on the basis of what they will look like in two or three years.

Freezing and thawing. The freezing and thawing that occur in northern climates can severely damage building materials. Wood decks can separate from their supports if not properly anchored. Roof structures will separate at the joints if improperly designed. These problems are often caused by water that runs into the joint cracks and expands when it freezes. The use of expansion joints, caulking, and proper weather protection of susceptible materials will reduce decay due to winter or wet-weather conditions.

CREATING THE DESIGN
The functional, site, and climatic considerations discussed above take into account the physical realities that influence your plans. The design ideas and methods discussed here offer the means for converting your needs and desires into working design solutions. The opportunity remains, at this point in the process, to modify or reevaluate your plan simply by altering your original criteria and their requirements.

Creating the design, once you have drawn up your mental shopping list, can be a rewarding experience. Now you can turn your ideas into reality. There are several ways in which to proceed. You can study the photographs of existing decks in this book. Or you can gather magazine photographs of deck designs, patterns, materials, and colors that appeal to you. Another way is to choose a specific design, commercially available or not, that can be modified to suit your own needs. Perhaps the most effective solution is to spell out all your requirements and with this list of objectives in mind, search for

designs and materials that best meet your needs.

The following design specifics will help you in this process.

Shape. What forms and shapes are compatible with your outdoor space? Select a familiar geometric shape such as a square, rectangle, triangle, hexagon, or circle for your deck. From the physical features of your site, you should be able to decide which of these shapes would best fit. Using this dominant geometry as the base, integrate other shapes around the main form. For example, if your deck site is predominantly rectangular, use a rectangle as the basic structural form and break up the rectangle into smaller shapes, or activity areas, such as squares, triangles, or smaller rectangles. Keep in mind that you are designing a space in which people will walk. Try to be as simple as possible while offering enough space for the different activities you want to accommodate.

Material compatibility. What materials will harmonize with the style of

your house? Your basic materials, textures, and colors should be in keeping with those of your house or the architecture of the surrounding area. While many possibilities are available, the choice of materials will strongly influence your design options.

Try to limit your selection to no more than two materials (see Chapter 2). Using a wide variety of materials can lead to overly complex and poorly executed construction. By restricting the number of materials you will have greater flexibility in the actual construction of the deck and in the final outfitting of the area.

Deck level. There are several types of construction to choose from, depending on the terrain of your site.

Deck on grade. This is suitable for a quite level site with a minimum of obstacles; a wood deck built just above grade is recommended. It is the least expensive because it usually requires little in the way of footings or posts. It is often built at or just below the interior floor level.

A deck on grade can be attached to

A DESIGN FOR A DECK AND PATIO

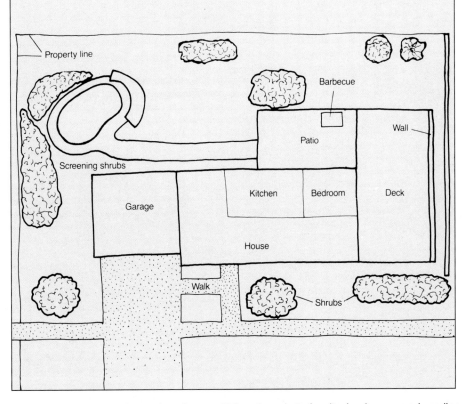

When your design ideas have taken shape, add them in scale to the site drawing you made earlier (page 21). Relationships between existing and proposed structures now appear.

the main house or it can be free-standing. Deciding which is the best often depends on the type of house construction and its material—wood is easy to join to; brick is much more difficult. A freestanding deck can be placed almost anywhere within a site and can reduce or eliminate the need for a connection to the house.

Raised deck, site sloping down from house. Where the terrain of the site you have selected slopes away from the house, you will have to support the deck above the sloping site. This requires posts and crossbracing to stabilize the deck. Access to the site is usually provided by exterior stairs. Building codes often require that a raised deck have two means of entrance or exit. A deck on a sloping site can step down in a series of platforms. A stepped deck is basically a combination of several smaller decks connected together. The complexity of construction, however, might deter you from creating a multi-level deck.

Two-story deck, site sloping up from house. Where the terrain rises away from the house, you can terrace the slope to the desired level. Thus the outer part of the deck will be on grade, and the rest can be elevated to this level. The deck should be accessible directly at the house level, rather than on a different level that requires steps up or down. Stepping out onto steps can be awkward, especially when carrying food, drink, and cooking supplies.

Deck with cantilevered construction. There are some sites that slope so steeply that you cannot support an extended deck on the site itself. The most obvious solution to this problem is to construct a cantilevered deck, one in which all supports are attached or connected to the house—nothing extends to the ground. This requires a much more complex design and building procedure than for a normal site construction, since the house must be capable of supporting the added load of the deck itself and the people and furniture placed on it. You should consult an architect, engineer, or contractor to work out the technical details required by this kind of construction. It is likely that much of the work will have to be done by professionals.

BASIC TYPES OF DECK CONSTRUCTION

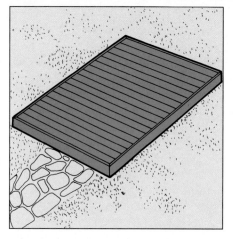

The simplest deck design rests directly on the ground, without any elaborate or expensive support structure.

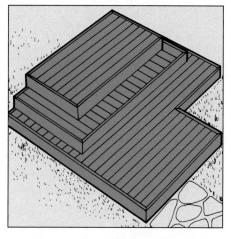

A visually more interesting form of simple deck combines ground-level sections with raised sections.

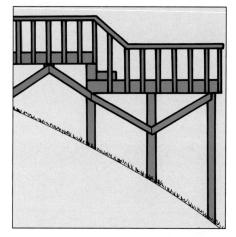

Deck construction adapts easily to sloping sites, provided post foundations are securely placed and posts are adequately braced.

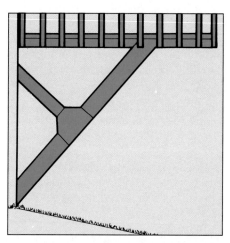

A deck may be cantilevered out from the second story of a house, without any ground support; professional advice is mandatory.

An elevated deck may be built on top of an existing building, using it for the necessary support structure.

A raised deck gains great stability by being attached on one side to a house; extended posts support the other side.

Access. Using your site analysis, you have already decided what type of deck to build. Consider also the best locations for access to the deck from the house and from other points on the site. You may want easy access from the kitchen, from the driveway or other parking space, or from walkways that lead to other parts of your property. On the other hand you may want a deck that is removed from the normal traffic pattern—one that offers privacy in a secluded corner. Another consideration is whether you want to put up fencing or walls. If so, where will they be located and to what extent do you want the deck set off from surroundings?

Adjacent, attached, or free-standing. A formal space arrangement is usually enhanced by a free-standing deck, whereas an informal arrangement works best for a deck built flush to the house. This decision is influenced by the main use you intend for the deck—formal entertaining or strictly informal family use. If you intend to use the deck for both these functions, you should plan your space to accommodate a variety of furniture layouts.

Roofings and coverings. Do you want a roof structure, awning, or other covering? Do you need partial or full coverage? Do you want the overhead covering to have the same shape as the deck? This subject is discussed in Chapter 10. In most cases you will place the overhead cover directly over the deck. You may choose to have support posts positioned within the interior of the deck; this involves planning and structural procedures discussed in Chapters 4, 5, and 6. Or you may place the support columns around the perimeter of the deck. In this case, size limitations may prevent you from providing cover for the entire deck. The dimension in one direction may be too long to be spanned on support columns placed outside the deck area.

Whatever your decision about overhead cover, you should plan the roofing structure so that the supports and overhead framing will be built first or at the same time as the deck structure. This will avoid conflicts between the structure required by the overhead supports

VARIETIES OF DECK DESIGN

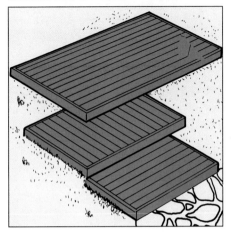

Low-level decks are simple to construct; multilevel design creates visual interest, while adapting to site requirements.

A free-standing deck can be as simple or as elaborate as you desire; wood construction can be varied easily to meet demands.

The most common deck design stands 2 to 4 feet off the ground, is attached on one side to a house, and includes stairs to reach the ground.

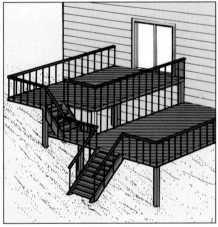

A steeply sloping site is no bar to deck construction. Multilevel decks are basically several simple decks standing together.

A raised deck can be built at practically any height if adequate support is provided by existing structures and strong posts with proper footings.

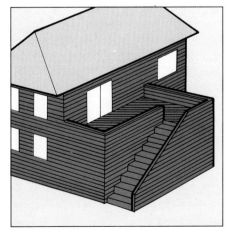

A deck and a house can be visually integrated by totally enclosing the deck structure with siding to match the main building.

and an already constructed deck. Remember that your local building code may contain specific requirements for overhead structures.

Landscaping. Building a deck will probably require additional landscaping. Although it is not absolutely necessary to finish landscaping at the same time as the deck is constructed, it is a good idea to decide how much landscaping will be required. In the plan of your deck, indicate the positions and types of flowers, shrubs and trees you'll be planting. Indicate both existing growth and the new materials you want to plant. A deck may be built at some distance away from the house in order to make room for a line of shrubs or plants to conceal an unsightly foundation, or to soften the overall effect of the house or other structures in the area.

Decorative elements. You may want to incorporate flower boxes, ornamental and reflecting pools, outdoor fireplaces, a barbecue, built-in seating, railings, stairs, as well as tree tubs or openings in the deck for trees to provide shade. You will need to gather visual samples and technical information for each of these elements. Try to integrate all of them into the geometry of your outdoor area, keeping the plan as simple as possible. If you intend to do all the construction work yourself, you need to select elements that are within your skills. If you intend to employ contractors, then the only limitations are space and money.

Patterns. Choose the type of decking pattern that is the most appropriate to your needs. Not only will different patterns require specific methods of material assembly, but a pattern that fits into the overall geometric scheme will make construction easier (see pages 36 and 42).

TYPES OF DECK OVERHEAD COVER

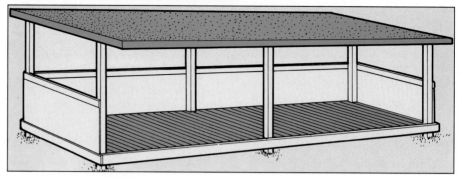

A solid roof gives a deck complete protection from rain, snow and sun, allowing deck use in almost all types of weather.

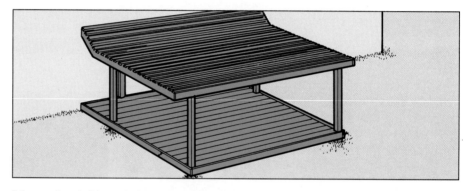

A louvered roof gives a deck partial shade without stopping rain. It also permits ventilation in hot seasons.

A trellis covered by vines makes a natural cover for a deck; it creates shade and some protection from rain. Flowers and fruits add visual interest.

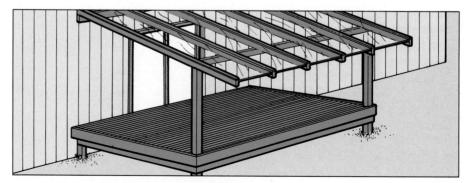

Transparent or translucent plastic sheets offer total protection from rain and snow, while letting in sunlight and heat.

2 DECK MATERIALS

The materials you select will strongly influence your deck design. There are many possible combinations. Some materials are more suitable for northern climates, others for southern climates. Wherever you live, select materials that are durable, pleasing to the eye, easy to obtain, relatively maintenance-free, easy to work with, and within your budget. Here are some suggestions to help you choose.

CHOOSING A DECK MATERIAL

A deck intended for do-it-yourself construction should use materials that are lightweight and capable of spanning small distances without excessive bending. A deck is either directly beside—and usually attached to—a house or is freestanding, away from a house. Except for cantilevered construction, a deck needs a foundation to support it in the ground, which requires two types of materials—one for the superstructure and another for the foundation. Keep the architecture, materials, and the decoration of your house in mind when choosing deck materials. If the materials of both house and deck are compatible, this will produce a natural transition between the interior of the house and the exterior deck.

The major criteria for selecting deck materials are these: They should be in keeping with the surrounding architecture. They should be available locally in pleasing colors and textures. They should require low maintenance and be economically feasible.

DECK SUPPORT MEMBERS

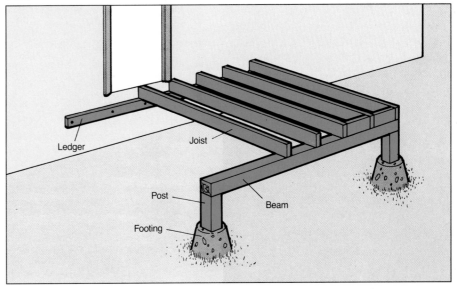

Most wood decks are supported by large-dimension lumber set on concrete footings. If the deck is attached to a house, one side rests on a ledger beam, eliminating a row of posts.

DECKING AND FINISHING ELEMENTS

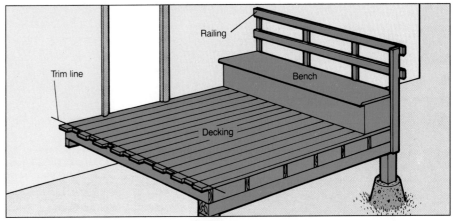

The visible parts of most decks include the decking, made of lengths of small lumber, plus railings, benches, and other elements added for user convenience.

WOOD

Wood is the most popular and basic deck material. The visual qualities of wood—its grain, texture, and color—make it an exciting material to work with.

Since all deck wood is used in an exterior application, it must have good weathering qualities and be free of rot and insect infestation. Cypress, spruce, and redwood possess excellent weathering durability, and if left unpainted will gradually acquire a soft, attractive, gray patina. Wood preservatives and pressure-treated wood, for exterior use, are available at lumberyards; their use will improve the durability of any deck.

The design possibilities offered by wood are endless; floorboard patterns, spacings, edgings, and railings all offer scope for your creative imagination. Wood construction patterns may appear complex, but they are fairly simple for a homeowner to build. Wood structural components are available in a variety of sizes, shapes, and textures. Local lumberyards display a wide range of materials to help you make a selection. Be sure to select wood that will weather to a desired color and patina. Newly installed wood looks very different from its later, weathered condition. Make sure you see samples of wood that has weathered in an exposure like the one your deck will experience. If you do not, you might be very disappointed in a few years. Wood can also be painted to integrate the deck with the color scheme of the house (wait six months before painting treated wood). Since the paint will cover most of the blemishes, a lower grade of material can be used. Wood can be fastened with a variety of connectors: nails, bolts, screws, and metal plates.

OTHER DECK MATERIALS

Most other deck materials require special building abilities. Metal decking or steel supports and grating are sometimes used, but the necessary cutting, hoisting, and welding would probably require an experienced contractor. Precast concrete floor panels require heavy machinery to install and, as with metal decks, the cost is quite high.

RECOMMENDED DIMENSION LUMBER GRADES

Building Uses	Appropriate Grades	Comments
Structural light framing 2–4″ thick 2–4″ wide	Select Structural No. 1 Appearance No. 2 Appearance	For lighter structural members, such as decking
Structural joists & planks 2–4″ thick 5″ and wider	Select Structural No. 1 Appearance No. 2 Appearance	For heavier structural members as indicated
Light framing 2–4″ thick 2–4″ wide	Construction	For use where high strength is not required; minimum grade for deck building

CHARACTERISTICS OF WOODS

Species	Bending strength	Post strength	Hardness	Heartwood resistance to decay	Resistance to warping	Holding paint	Holding nails	Ease of working
Redwood	2	1	2	1	1	1	2	2
Cypress	2	2	2	1	2	1	2	2
Western cedar	3	2	3	1	1	1	3	1
Spruce	2	2	3	3	2	2	2	2
Southern pine	1	1	2	2	2	3	1	2
Other pines	3	3	3	3	1	1	3	1
Douglas fir	1	1	2	2	2	3	1	2
Hemlock	2	2	2	3	2	3	3	2

Key: 1-relatively high, 2-intermediate, 3-relatively low

LUMBER SIZES

Nominal	Actual	Nominal	Actual	Nominal	Actual
1×2	¾″ × 1½″	1×10	¾″ × 9¼″	2×8	1½″ × 7¼″
1×3	¾″ × 2½″	1×12	¾″ × 11¼″	2×10	1½″ × 9¼″
1×4	¾″ × 3½″	2×2	1½″ × 1½″	2×12	1½″ × 11¼″
1×6	¾″ × 5½″	2×3	1½″ × 2½″	4×4	3½″ × 3½″
1×8	¾″ × 7¼″	2×4	1½″ × 3½″	6×6	5½″ × 5½″
		2×6	1½″ × 5½″		

These are industry standards for dry lumber. Green lumber is slightly larger, e.g., a green 2 × 4 is 1⁹⁄₁₆″ × 3⁹⁄₁₆″. Green lumber may be easier to work with, but it is more likely to warp and split. Let green lumber dry for 3 to 4 weeks.

STRENGTH RATINGS OF WOOD SPECIES

Group I (strongest)	Group II	Group III
Douglas fir	Western cedar	Non-southern pine
Western hemlock	Douglas fir (southern)	Redwood
Western larch	White fir	Non-coast Sitka spruce
Southern pine	Eastern hemlock	Northern white spruce
Coast Sitka spruce		

Ratings refer to lumber grade No. 1 or better.

RECOMMENDED MAXIMUM DECKING SPANS

Species	1 × 4, 1 × 6 flat	2 × 3, 2 × 4 flat	2 × 4 on edge
Group I	16″	60″	144″
Group II	14″	48″	120″
Group III	12″	42″	108″

Recommendations apply to dimension and board lumber.

DECK ROOF STRUCTURES

A roof structure allows you to further define the outdoor living area. A roof with an overhang can extend the area of the deck; it can vary the height in relation to the house, or extend the deck area to encompass additional space such as walkways.

Gazebo. A gazebo is a small, roofed structure. It may be freestanding adjacent to a deck or may be constructed at one corner, using the deck as a floor. The traditional gazebo provides the feeling of a separate enclosed area while allowing light to filter through. Precut gazebos are widely available.

Trellis. A horizontal trellis can be supported by vertical posts to form an open latticework roof over a deck. A freestanding overhead trellis must be completely supported by posts; an attached trellis uses the house for support on one side and posts at the other side. A trellis is usually built from narrow pine or fir stock applied to a wood frame.

A trellis or other overhead structure can support climbing plants that act as a sunscreen, providing shade and visual privacy and at the same time helping to control air movement. It also provides protection from external noise.

MATERIALS FOR DECK ROOFS

Wood is the most commonly used deck roofing material because it is relatively lightweight, cost-competitive, and easy to work with. Its texture, warm color, and pattern combined with solid stability account for its popularity.

Most wood roof structures are limited in span—the distance between supports for a horizontal beam. Such crosspieces must support not only their own weight without sagging over the years, but also the weight of pieces attached to them as well as the roof covering or overhead plant growth. As a result, a wood roof is usually composed of one or more small units, or modules, of stable structural design; you may increase the number of modules as needed. Some of the species used most often are redwood, cypress, spruce, hemlock, pine, and fir. As with materials for the deck itself, it is advisable to purchase wood that is already treated for exterior use.

TYPES OF DECK ROOF STRUCTURES

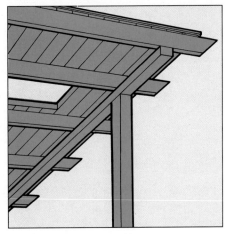
A lightweight wood roof, made of the same materials as the deck, provides shade and protection from rain.

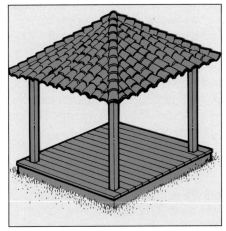
A tile roof gives the deck structure a more substantial appearance; it requires stronger support members.

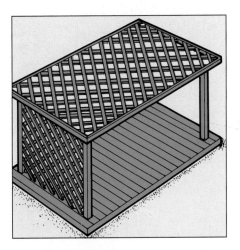
A covering of thin lath provides only a minimum of shade and rain protection, but creates an air of privacy.

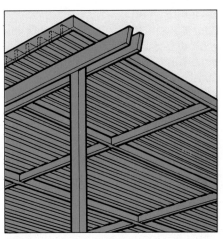
Narrow boards set on edge create more shade than a lath roof, but hardly any protection from rain.

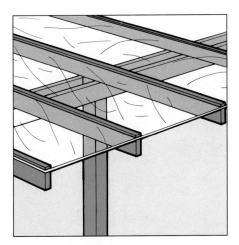
Sheets of clear plastic give complete rain protection, while flooding the deck with all the available light.

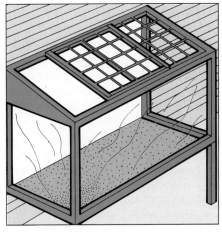
Glass windows on all sides of a deck create a solarium. Sliding windows of safety glass above permit ventilation on warm days.

Lath. Pieces of lath can be set into a crosspiece or nailed directly to the supporting members in a crisscross or diagonal pattern for an openwork deck roof.

Louvers. Horizontal wood slats, similar to those in a wood blind or shutter, are usually available in prefabricated units. They are unfinished and suitable for exterior use.

Reed and bamboo. The visual effect of reed and bamboo is quite elegant. They can be cut into equal lengths and tied to the superstructure with rope. The quality of light filtered through reed or bamboo is particularly pleasant. Unfortunately, since they deteriorate rapidly, these materials must be replaced often.

Canvas. Canvas panels laced or tacked to a frame create a light and summery feeling. They give shade from the sun and protection from the wind and rain. Canvas is moderately priced and widely available. It comes in many weights and colors, is easily cut and bound, and adds vivid touches of color not found in natural materials. Canvas, stretched on a wood frame, can be hung from a roof structure to make an effective temporary screen. However, it must be replaced often.

Plastic panels. Corrugated or flat plastic panels are sold in a variety of thicknesses and colors. The standard size is two feet wide and six to eight feet long. The panels can be cut with simple home tools. Other advantages are that plastic panels can easily be set into a wood frame, provide a soft, diffused light, withstand the effects of weather except extreme cold, are easy to maintain, and are relatively inexpensive.

Metal. There are many lightweight metal panels sold for use as inset roofing material or as spanning elements. Corrugated aluminum or steel panels come in many lengths, gauges, and colors. They are strong and are easily cut and installed. They are relatively maintenance-free and inexpensive, and provide complete shade control and protection from rain. But metal panels expand and contract a significant amount in hot weather, which can make annoying noises or cause separation at the panel connections unless they are properly prepared.

LIGHTWEIGHT DECK COVERS

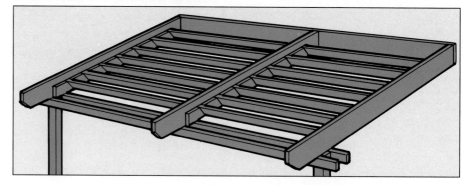

Thin boards mounted at an angle make a louvered cover that creates shade but still allows wind and rain to reach the deck.

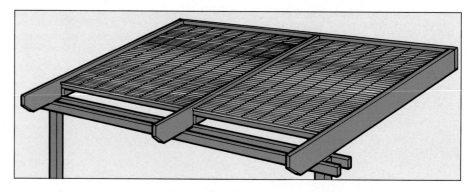

Long pieces of reed or bamboo, tied together in flexible sheets, can be mounted on a very light framework. Different qualities of shade are created by varying the density of the sheets.

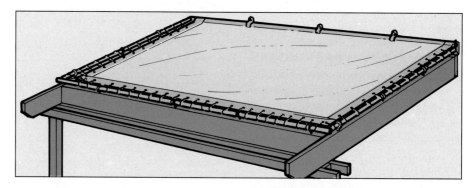

Canvas laced through grommets to an aluminum pipe frame provides excellent shade. A pipe running through a tunnel stitched in the canvas is held to the house by C-shaped conduit clamps.

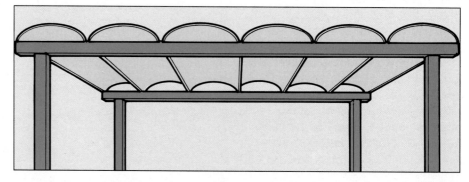

Plastic panels, relatively inexpensive to buy and install, provide protection from rain while flooding the deck with light. Darker colored panels hold back glaring sun.

STRUCTURAL CHARACTERISTICS OF WOOD

Wood is prized for its durability and structural capabilities. It has high resistance to impact and high strength in compression relative to its weight. It can be worked easily into many shapes without seriously altering its behavioral characteristics. Wood does, however, have natural defects such as knots, splits, and checks. It can also suffer shrinkage, decay, and warping.

Wood is available throughout the United States, but the availability of particular species depends on geographical location. The cost of wood remains generally stable but may increase with demand. Wood used in deck, fence, and roofing construction is referred to as "lumber." Lumber is produced by saw and planing mills in standard sizes and with characteristics that can be guaranteed by the manufacturer. This uniformity of size, strength, and stability assures you that the material you buy will behave in a predictable manner.

Species. Wood is divided into two groups. Softwoods such as fir, hemlock, red and white cedar, spruce, redwood, and pine are found in most geographic regions. More than half the available lumber used for decks, fences, and roofing is softwood, as is most of the lumber used for wood-frame house construction.

Hardwoods include maple, oak, elm, birch, ash, cherry, walnut, poplar, and hickory. Hardwoods are normally used only for interior paneling and furniture because they are expensive and difficult to obtain. They are known for the visual appeal of their grain, color, and texture. Hardwoods are more likely to change in size due to the effects of moisture.

Decay and expansion. Wood is composed almost entirely of cells that are bound together by a natural glue that gives it strength. The cells, however, are subject to natural decay. Most lumber available is heartwood, cut from the center of the tree, which is less likely to decay than sapwood. The porosity of wood, due to its cell structure, causes the cells to swell as moisture is absorbed and to contract when the wood dries out. The expansion of

TYPES OF WOOD GRAIN AND DEFECTS

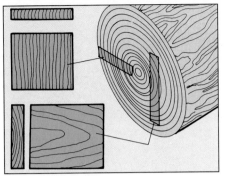

The board at top left is quarter-sawn; the board at the bottom is plain-sawn.

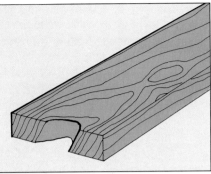

Large or medium-size knots in boards are undesirable, especially if they are loose and likely to fall out.

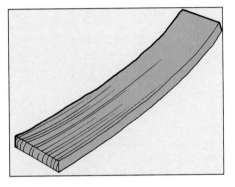

Bowing is a lengthwise bending of a board caused by uneven shrinking.

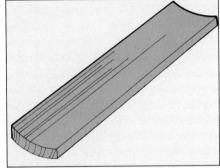

Cupping is a crosswise bending of a board caused by uneven shrinking.

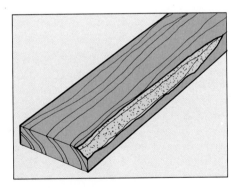

A wane is a severe defect in which a large section of one edge drops off.

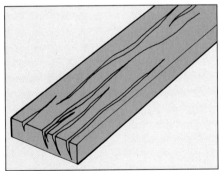

Splits and cracks severely weaken a board, as well as spoil its appearance.

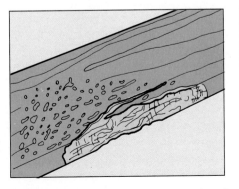

Decay and honeycomb rot render a board useless for construction purposes.

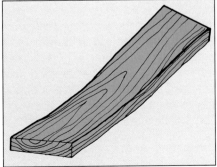

A moderate twist may not weaken a board, but it does make it undesirable for finishing.

lumber used in an exterior deck might be a concern in areas with a high moisture level in the air. Moisture in wood reduces its strength and affects its size and ability to successfully accept paint and stain.

Grading. All lumber is graded according to certain visual characteristics. The grading is a measure of the overall quality of the wood. Some of the visual defects that influence grading are knots, which indicate the position of branches in the trunk (lesser grades can have more knots than select grades) and shakes, which are separations along the long grain. Pitch pockets indicate a grain separation in the short end grain.

Lumber grades. While there are many lumber grades, most of the lumber recommended for deck, fence, and roofing construction need not be any better than No. 2 Common. The Western Wood Products Association (WWPA) has standardized the grading of all lumber in this order:

Select Structural: the best and strongest, but most expensive.

No. 1 Appearance: sound, tight-knotted lumber with few defects; not readily available; recommended for decks.

No. 2 Appearance: may contain a few defects such as loose knots; no knotholes or major defects are allowed; recommended for deck construction.

No. 3 Appearance: not recommended for decks; will contain more defects than No. 2, including open knotholes.

Construction: minimum grade recommended for deck construction.

Standard, Utility, Stud: these grades are not recommended for deck construction.

In addition to the above grades, such terms as Common and Select are used to differentiate between wood used for framing and general construction and that used for wood trim. While a better quality of material such as No. 2 or Construction grade might initially be more expensive, your investment will guarantee a sturdier and longer lasting deck or roof.

Curvature. Almost all lumber sold today is plain sawn. This is true of all

RECOMMENDED STRUCTURAL DIMENSIONS

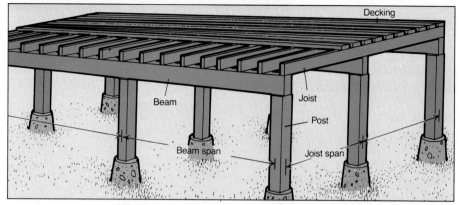

The dimensions of your deck must be drawn up with the strength of your lumber in mind. Check with the lumberyard first as to availability and cost; then use the charts below for planning.

RECOMMENDED MAXIMUM JOIST SPANS

Joist size	Species	16" spacing	24" spacing	32" spacing
2×6	Group I	9'9"	8'6"	7'9"
	Group II	8'7"	7'6"	6'10"
	Group III	7'9"	6'9"	6'2"
2×8	Group I	12'10"	11'3"	10'2"
	Group II	11'4"	9'11"	9'0"
	Group III	10'2"	8'11"	8'1"
2×10	Group I	16'5"	14'4"	13'0"
	Group II	14'6"	12'8"	11'6"
	Group III	13'0"	11'4"	10'4"

Example: A 2×8 joist from Group II, using 24" joist spacing, should span no more than 9'11".

The groups of tree species are listed on page 30. Decide on actual deck dimensions after you have selected the type of lumber.

RECOMMENDED BEAM SPANS (length of beam between posts)

Species Group	Beam Size	Distance between Posts
		4' · 5' · 6' · 7' · 8' · 9' · 10' · 11'
Group I	4×6	Up to 6'
	3×8	Up to 8' — 7' — 6'
	4×8	Up to 10' — 9' — 8' — 7' — 6'
	3×10	Up to 11' — 10' — 9' — 8' — 7' — 6'
	4×10	Up to 12' — 11' — 10' — 9' — 8' — 7'
	3×12	Up to 12' — 11' — 10' — 9' — 8'
	4×12	Up to 12' — 11' — 10' — 9'
Group II	4×6	Up to 6'
	3×8	Up to 7' — 6'
	4×8	Up to 9' — 8' — 7' — 6'
	3×10	Up to 10' — 9' — 8' — 7' — 6'
	4×10	Up to 11' — 10' — 9' — 8' — 7'
	3×12	Up to 12' — 11' — 10' — 9' — 8' — 7'
	4×12	Up to 12' — 11' — 10' — 9' — 8'
Group III	4×6	Up to 6'
	3×8	Up to 7' — 6'
	4×8	Up to 8' — 7' — 6'
	3×10	Up to 9' — 8' — 7' — 6'
	4×10	Up to 10' — 9' — 8' — 7' — 6'
	3×12	Up to 11' — 10' — 9' — 8' — 7' — 6'
	4×12	Up to 12' — 11' — 10' — 9' — 8' — 7'

Example: If the beams are set on posts 8' apart, and the lumber is from Group I, a 3×8 beam can span up to 6'. Recommendations apply to lumber grade No. 2 or better.

The groups of tree species are listed on page 30. Find out what lumber is available before drawing up your actual deck dimensions.

lumber available for framing and decking. (Quarter sawing, in which the log is cut in a diagonal fashion so that the wood will be uniform in shrinkage, is used only for hardwoods.) As a result, most lumber has an end grain that can cause the piece to curve. Make sure that all decking boards curve downward by installing them bark-side up. This will prevent cupping. Look at the end of the board to determine the right side; place the concave side down.

Strength. Wood strength is determined by cell wall thickness and adhesion between cells along the length of the piece. Lumber strength is greatest parallel to the grain; there is less strength perpendicular to the grain.

Lumber sizes. All lumber is sold in nominal, or identifying, sizes, as opposed to the actual measured sizes. A chart on page 30 lists the standard sizes currently in use in the industry. As the chart shows, a nominal 2 × 4 is actually smaller than 2 inches by 4 inches. The chart lists all the sizes you will use and that are necessary for building a wood deck, fence, or roof structure. There are a great many more sizes, but they are not generally used for this scale of construction.

Each lumber size can support a specified weight, which varies with the spacing, species used, span distance, and the method of connection used. Most building codes specify the load that any deck must be able to carry. Based on these requirements, the beam and joist sizes given in the charts on the opposite page are conservative recommendations.

For spans of more than 14 feet, consult with a lumber dealer or a structural engineer. All the size and span data in these charts take into account normal deck loadings. If you plan to place very heavy objects, such as concrete planters or a hot tub on your deck, the data in the charts are not applicable.

The distance that the main structural beams have to span is determined by the spacing of the supporting posts or piers; the longer the span, the heavier the beam needed. The distance the joists or smaller beams have to span is determined by the distance between the beams, and the size and spacing are calculated accordingly. The joist

WOOD PRESERVATION

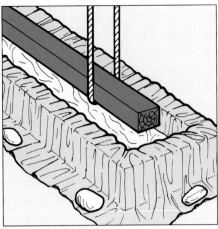

If you cannot buy pressure-treated wood, treat all lumber with preservatives. Soak pieces in a plastic-lined bath as the manufacturer directs.

A good way to treat posts is to soak them in preservative solution for 24 hours, using a 50- or 100-gallon metal drum.

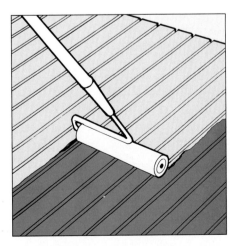

Preservatives should be applied to the decking before or immediately after construction, and renewed every year or so as needed.

span table is based on normal bending limits; after all, you don't want a deck to bounce or to flex like a diving board every time you walk across it.

The posts that support the beams, which in turn support the joists that carry the decking, are 4 × 4 timber posts for heights of up to 6 feet above the ground; these posts can be placed no farther apart than 6 feet on center. For heights from 6 feet to 12 feet above grade, 6 × 6 timber posts should be used, placed no more than 10 feet apart on center. These sizes ensure a safe load transfer from the posts to the foundation; they are also adequate to support overhead cover.

Decking. Wood decking comes in several sizes and species. Do not use decking wider than 6 inches. Using narrower widths minimizes cupping and the potential for splitting along the board. Normally, 2 × 6 wood decking will span a joist spacing of 4 feet. 2 × 4 decking will span 3 feet if laid on its side and run for more than two joist spaces. Most 1 × 4 and 1 × 6 decking will span no more than 16 inches without flexing when laid flat and continued over more than two spans. In any case, the shorter the span, the stiffer the deck. If you plan to have unusual loads on the deck, such as heavy furniture, these recommendations are not applicable; in this case, you should call in an architect or contractor.

Wood preservation. The best way to get lumber that is free from decay is to buy only grades that exclude decay. Wood, like any natural material, attracts insects, fungi, mold, and stains. To secure lumber free of these faults, buy only material with a moisture content of less than 20 percent. Most lumber for home construction is sold with a 16 percent moisture content. One way to minimize rot is to keep wood away from sources of moisture. This will also help to prevent insects from boring into it. Almost all wood used today requires some form of preservative or protective coating. Lumber used in exterior applications especially needs protection against insects and decay. A pressure-injected lumber preservative provides the most effective protection.

Pressure-treated wood especially for

use in exterior decks, fences, and other exposed structures is available at most lumberyards. Its primary advantage is that you do not have to treat it by spraying, soaking, or brushing with preservatives. If you can buy pressure-treated exterior lumber, by all means do so.

The chemicals used to treat lumber are water-soluble preservatives containing a form of chromated copper arsenate or ammoniacal copper arsenate. These odorless compounds do not stain or discolor. Wood preservatives are essential for the satisfactory performance of the deck. They are well worth the small extra cost.

Deck patterns. Some common wood deck patterns are shown at the right. Patterns in which long segments are laid parallel and at right angles to the joists are of course the easiest to install. Diagonal deck patterns, laid at a 45 degree angle to the joists, provide variety in deck appearance, give visual direction to the deck, or add aesthetic interest. When decking is laid on a diagonal the joist spacing will have to be reduced to compensate for the longer span. Herringbone, zigzag, or radial patterns may look too busy.

If you want a more free-form design, you can install almost any pattern imaginable as long as you maintain the decking and joist arrangement previously discussed. Where a change in the direction of the decking occurs, a double joist must be laid parallel to the cut line for reinforcement. With a herringbone or diamond pattern on a 48-inch or smaller grid, blocking must be added to support each change of direction. The direction change should be made over joists or beams, to provide adequate support.

Framing around a tree. When laying decking around a tree, try to keep the pattern as simple as possible. If your pattern requires unusual footing requirements, digging into the roots of the tree should be avoided at all costs. Plan the framing so that there is ample clearance around the tree, especially a young or fast-growing one. The higher the deck is off the ground, the more the tree will sway and so the larger the deck opening will have to be. Plan on enough room so that tree and deck can coexist comfortably.

TYPES OF DECKING PATTERNS

Almost any design for the decking is possible. However, the more elaborate the design, the more work involved, especially in providing adequate joist support for all decking pieces.

FRAMING A TREE

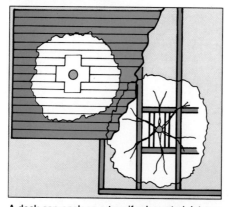

A deck can enclose a tree if adequate joist support is provided for all decking. Allow room for wind sway as well as growth.

TYPES OF DECKING

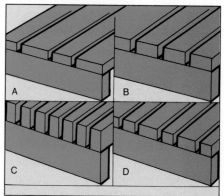

A: Alternating 2 × 4s and 2 × 6s, laid flat. B: 2 × 4s laid flat. C: 2 × 4s on edge. D: alternating 2 × 2s and 2 × 4s laid flat.

3 DEVELOPING A SITE PLAN

Design ideas must be drawn out clearly so that you can obtain the necessary building permits and estimate the quantities of materials and supplies needed to build the deck. The first step is to create a measured drawing of the site, including the existing structures, lot lines, easements, underground utilities, water lines, and, of course, the proposed deck. The procedure is simple but requires a methodical and consistent approach to recording accurately what exists on the site. First, buy some 8½ × 11-inch, or larger, grid paper, also called graph paper. The grid is usually light blue printed on white background. You'll need a yardstick, carpenter's folding rule, or a 12-foot tape measure, in order to establish the dimensions of structures, distances on the site, and the position of trees and shrubs. Mount the grid paper on a clipboard or other firm support so that it will stay in place. Now you are ready to start working out your site plan.

DRAWING THE PLAN

Follow these steps in drawing up your plan.

1. Mark, in an upper page corner, the North arrow, plus East, West, and South. Mark the directions from which the prevailing summer and winter winds blow.

2. Select an outside corner of your house at the foundation line as the reference point for all subsequent measurements. From this corner, measure the dimensions and locations of all ex-

DRAWING A SITE PLAN

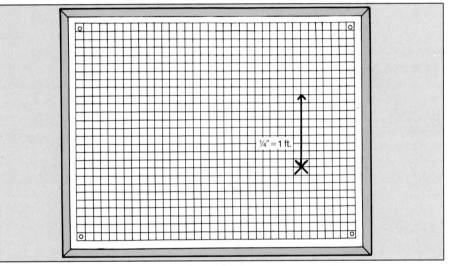

1. Use a large sheet of grid paper. Decide what scale you will use; a ¼ inch on the paper equaling 1 foot on the ground is standard. X marks the house corner where measuring starts.

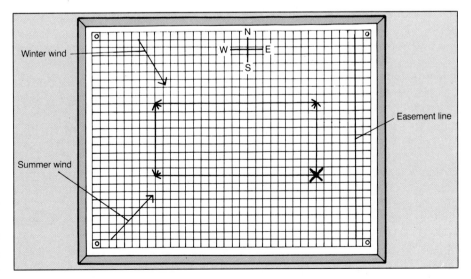

2. Mark the orientation of your plan; north is usually at the top. Measure the dimensions of your house and other structures and mark them on the paper, beginning at the X.

isting and proposed structures and plantings to be plotted on the grid.

3. Establish a drawing scale by setting a value of ¼, ½, 1, or 2 feet for each grid square. If you use a scale of ¼ inch equal to 1 foot, then a measurement of 10 feet along your foundation wall would be marked 10 grid squares long on your plan. Choose a scale that will put your entire plan on no more than one or two sheets of grid paper.

4. Measure the entire foundation of your house and draw it on the grid. Mark north, south, east, and west exposures.

5. Locate the interior room that will connect with the deck. Measure from the original reference corner around the outside of the house until you come to a window, door, or joint that is also part of that room. Measure the room dimensions from that point and mark them on the scale drawing.

6. From the information gathered from local utilities, mark down the positions of all pipes and wires. This will reveal any conflict between your deck design ideas and any underground or overhead utilities.

7. Next, mark the boundaries and corners of your property. You may have to add some paper to include your entire lot drawn to scale. Mark the lot lines, the setback lines that local zoning requires, and any easements that are part of your deed.

8. Mark the positions of all trees and shrubs that will be kept and those that will have to be removed or relocated. This will indicate the shady areas and help in estimating the amount of landscaping work required. Make several copies of this plan so you can try more than one deck design and layout.

9. Now draw in the plan of the proposed deck, including stairs, railings, supports for overhead cover, and any other elements. It is helpful to compare several plan arrangements, drawn on various copies of your original site plan, so that you can visualize the size and shape possibilities and begin to estimate quantities and types of materials needed. Now is the time to discover potential problems with your plan. Be sure the spacing of posts, beams, and joists follows the recommendations given on page 34.

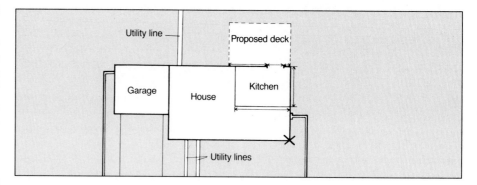

3. Mark the interior dimensions of rooms that will connect with the proposed deck. Mark the location of utility lines that must be avoided when digging.

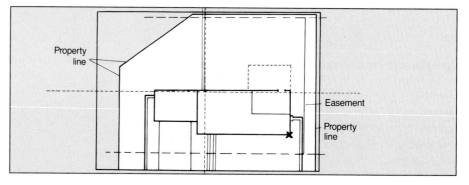

4. Mark property lines, easements, and any building restriction imposed by your local building codes. Setbacks from property lines may be very specific.

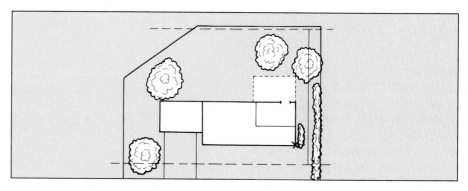

5. Mark the location of existing trees and plantings and specify which ones are to be kept and which will be removed. Indicate proposed plantings.

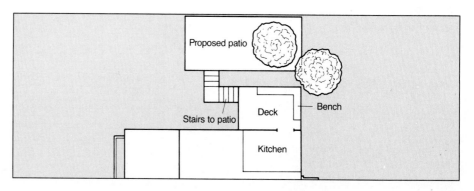

6. Draw in the proposed deck, scaled accurately to size, including steps, railings, pathways, and any other elements, so that you can begin to visualize the completed project.

Once you are settled on your design, draw up the plan at a larger scale, perhaps 1 inch equal to 1 foot. To do this, simply convert all previous measurements to the new scale. For example, if you measured 10 feet on the ground, that would convert to 40 grid squares on your plan at the larger scale. This drawing can be limited to the deck and the immediate area, including portions of the house and other structures or significant features, such as a pool or paths. Also include trees, flower beds, and shrubs. This larger scale plan will help you visualize the patterns of your design as well as the relative size of the project.

MAKING AN ON-THE-GROUND CHECK

Now that you have drawn up a plan with all the elements indicated, it is a good idea to take your plan, some stakes, a ball of twine, and a hammer, and lay out your deck plan on the ground. Take a good look at it. Bring out some furniture and place it within the proposed deck area. You may find that the dimensions are too confining. Now is the time to change. Mark down final dimensions, as well as the materials you'll be using, on your scale plan.

DRAWING THE ELEVATION

After you have made a plan of your deck at a scale large enough for all the details to be indicated, you are ready to draw an elevation—a vertical picture at the same large scale.

If your deck is attached to the house, measure vertically from a horizontal line on your foundation or from a floor line that shows on the outside, to find the height of all openings, vents, eaves, roof lines, and such. Mark these, as well as the ground level, on your scale elevation. If your deck is not connected to the house, indicate only the ground level.

Add an elevation drawing (side view) of your proposed deck, including railings, stairs, and connections to other structures, that you plan to build. All this information is necessary for estimating material needs.

Most building inspectors and the local building departments that grant permits will accept a well-drawn plan and elevation of the type described above with your application for a permit. If they require a more architectural plan, a local drafting service or an architectural firm can provide the necessary help.

ESTIMATING MATERIALS AND SUPPLIES

Use the completed plans of your proposed deck to make a list of all materials and supplies needed. Include the quantities and dimensions of each size of lumber; for example, 12 4 × 4 8-foot posts, 36 2 × 6 10-foot joists. Since there is some waste when installing decking and railings, add about 5 percent to your estimate of materials for these components. For example, if you figure you need 38 2 × 4s, buy two or three extra to be on the safe side.

Include post footings, cement mix, fasteners (nails, bolts, and screws), connectors (joist hangers, post anchors), and any wood preservatives and stains that you'll need.

When calculating lumber quantities, remember that while you draw up plans in actual dimensions, you buy lumber in nominal sizes (see chart on page 30). For example, on your plan a joist may actually measure $1\frac{1}{2} \times 9\frac{1}{4}$ inches, but at the lumberyard it is a 2 × 10.

Use the following method to estimate the quantity of decking you'll need. Find the number of 2 × 4s needed to fill a given deck width by multiplying the deck width in feet by 3.4. (The deck width is the dimension of the deck that is at right angles to the direction in which the 2 × 4s are laid.) For example, to fill 12 feet of deck width with 2 × 4s, figure 12 × 3.4 = 40 (rounded off) plus 5 percent for waste = about 43. If your deck is 16 feet long, you need 43 16-foot 2 × 4s. However, 2 × 4s are sold in 6, 8, and 12-foot lengths. In this case, you would buy about 86 8-foot 2 × 4s. If you plan to use 2 × 6s for your deck flooring, use a factor of 2.1 instead of 3.4 to find the number of pieces needed.

When you are ready to buy lumber, keep in mind that a lumberyard offers the largest selection of lumber sizes, species, and grades, but it may not

JOIST AND DECKING DETAILS

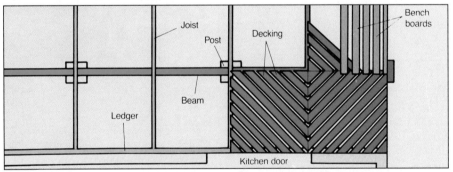

When you draw your plan in large scale, indicate all the posts, beams and joists, as well as a portion of the decking design. The ends of all decking pieces must have joist support.

A DECK ELEVATION DRAWING

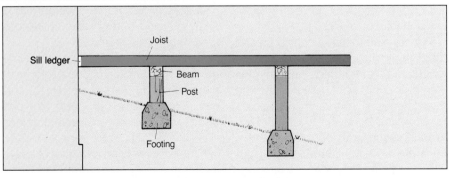

A large-scale elevation drawing of your deck plan shows all the elements from the side. Be sure to indicate any slope of the site, so that post height can be calculated accurately.

stock a large variety of fasteners and other supplies. A home center or building materials outlet will stock what you need. Many stores will give personalized service: drawings, materials lists, costs, and suggestions. Shopping around will reveal the best deal.

Some suppliers price lumber by the linear foot; that is, a one-foot-long piece of whatever type or size you need. Other suppliers sell by the board foot, which is a quantity of wood 1 foot long by 1 foot wide by 1 inch thick. In this case, the price will be for 1,000 board feet of the size and type you want.

To estimate the board footage of your decking, multiply the nominal width of the decking in inches by the nominal thickness in inches by the actual length of one piece in inches. Multiply this result by the number of pieces required and divide the answer by 144. (See lumber size chart, page 30.)

DECIDING WHO WILL BUILD THE DECK

When you have finished the plans for your deck and obtained the permits—but before you buy any materials—you should decide who will build the deck. If you have basic carpentry skills and the necessary tools (see page 46) and are willing to invest the time and labor, you and a helper can build any simple deck on an ordinary site. The savings in labor costs will be substantial.

However, if your plans call for a deck raised more than 6 or 8 feet off the ground, or built on unstable or steeply sloping ground, or over water, or cantilevered out from a second floor, or requiring any other complicated construction, you should hire a competent contractor to do the job. Local building codes may require that a professional build a retaining wall, for example, or install electrical wiring.

If you decide to hire a contractor, get three competitive bids, check each contractor's references, and inspect examples of his work. Ask people who have hired the contractor to evaluate his work and behavior. And, most important, secure a written contract with anyone you hire; it should spell out the project in detail as to materials, schedules, and payment. Never rely on verbal agreements.

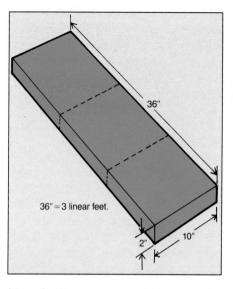

A linear foot is a 12″ length of any nominal dimension size of lumber. This is 3 linear feet of 2 × 10.

A board foot is a volume measurement: 144 cubic inches. Thus, 36″ of 2 × 10 is 5 board feet.

DECK DESIGNS THAT NEED PROFESSIONAL HELP

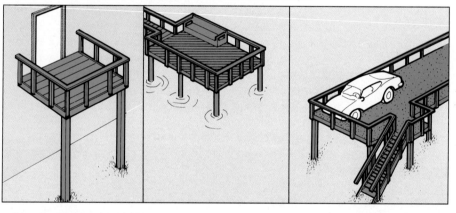

If you plan to build a deck standing more than 8 feet off the ground (left), that stands in water (center), or that will carry heavy loads (right), get professional design assistance.

CHECKLIST

This list summarizes the decisions and initiatives you must take to successfully complete a deck building project.

1. Decide what functions you want your deck to fulfill; gather appropriate design ideas (see pages 17–19).

2. Make note of site considerations (view, privacy) and climatic influences (see pages 19–20 and 23–25).

3. Learn how local zoning ordinances and building codes might influence your plan (see page 21).

4. Examine your property title and deed for any easements or restrictions contained therein (see pages 21–22).

5. Get copies of any architect's drawings and maps of your property.

6. Draw preliminary sketches (see pages 21 and 25).

7. Make scale drawings of the plan and elevation (see pages 37–39). You may want to employ an architect, landscape architect, or designer at this point to finalize plans.

8. Take drawings to the local building department to secure permits, or to obtain information about any revisions required.

9. Make lists of materials required and do some comparison shopping (see pages 39–40).

10. Decide whether to hire a contractor or to do the whole job or part of it yourself (see this page).

11. Visit your bank to arrange for financing, if necessary.

12. Purchase materials and supplies; begin construction (see Chapter 5).

13. Have inspectors check the work in progress, as required by local law.

4 DECK BUILDING BASICS

Before starting the construction of a deck project, identify clearly all those pieces that will make up the finished deck. Every deck consists of two major sections: 1. Above-grade elements such as decking, joists, beams, ledgers, railings, and deck furniture; 2. Below-grade or supporting elements such as posts or piers, footings, and foundations. In addition to the lumber for these elements, you also need fasteners and connectors to hold them together and the tools to do the job.

PARTS OF A DECK

All weights and loads that are imposed on a deck are directly supported by the decking. While the decking might appear to be decorative, its main function is to transfer all the weight and load to the joists. Joists are the primary structural element supporting the deck floor. They are best described as closely spaced structural members that support the deck and which in turn are supported by horizontal beams. The beams are larger elements that gather the load and weight of the joists resting on them and transfer it to the posts. The posts are vertical supports spaced at appropriate intervals to transfer all the load from the beams directly into the ground through the footings. Footings, which bear all the weight of the deck, are set into the soil to distribute the weight uniformly. In low-profile

ESSENTIAL PARTS OF A DECK

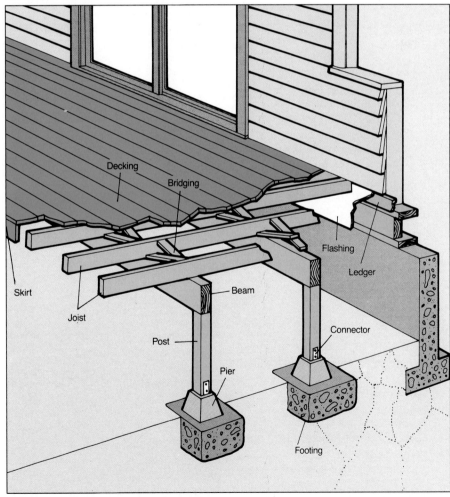

Standard wood deck construction uses the parts shown here, arranged so that the decking—the visible component—is supported by larger and more widely spaced members, including joists, beams, posts, piers, and at the bottom, footings. The ledger beam secures one side of the deck to an existing structure.

decks built very near the ground, the beams themselves may rest on the footings, thus eliminating the need for posts.

Decking. The major visual element of a deck is the decking, the surface you stand on. It is the most interesting part of the deck because of its pattern and detailing. The decking pattern also determines the spacing of the joists, which in turn affects the beams and the footings. Therefore, the pattern you select must be coordinated with a suitable structural framing plan. Most wood decking can be applied in many patterns, the most common being parallel, diagonal, diamond, radial, and parquet. The most-often-used grade of lumber is No. 2 Common (see chart on page 30). The most popular species used for decking are redwood, cedar, hemlock, fir, and pine. In order to satisfy local building codes for exterior decks, all decking should be supported by joists no farther apart than 24 inches on center. If you plan to have heavy weights on the decking, the spacing should be 16 inches on center.

Almost all decking material is laid flat; that is, on its broad side. This means that the 2-inch nominal dimension of the decking is the depth, and the 4- or 6-inch dimension is the wearing surface. For a finer-lined, more narrowly patterned deck, you can set the 2×4s on edge instead of flat. Of course, more material will be used, at greater expense.

Decking boards are usually spaced about ⅛ to ¼ inch apart to let rain and dirt pass through to the ground.

Because the layout of the decking determines the layout of the supporting structure, first choose the deck pattern you want, then the grade of material and the type, and finally the spacing of the joists.

Joists. The joists bear the full brunt of the load from the decking. They are supported at each end (and perhaps in the middle) by beams and they span the space between the beams. Joist spacing is usually dictated by the spanning and load-bearing capacity of the joist rather than by spacing imposed by the decking. The chart on page 34 gives joist span limits for different sizes of joists. Most joists are 2-inch wood

VARIATIONS OF DECKING PATTERNS

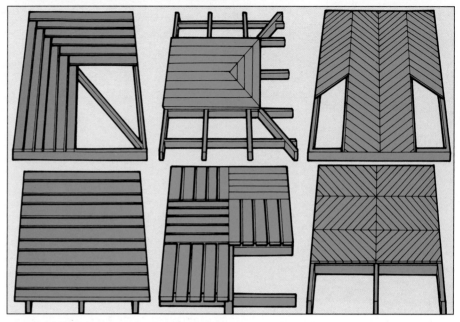

Decking materials can be laid down in almost any desired pattern, as long as sufficient support is provided by underlying joists, especially at the ends of the decking pieces.

METHODS OF SPACING DECKING

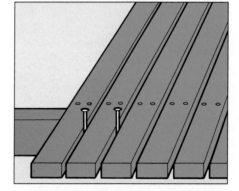

The most common method of installing decking is to lay 2×4s on their wide sides and nail them to the joists. Large nails provide temporary spacing.

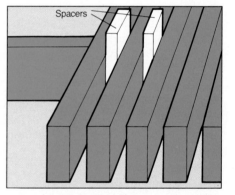

Another method of installing 2×4 decking is to set the pieces on edge and toenail them in place, using thin scraps of wood as spacers.

DECKING JOINTS

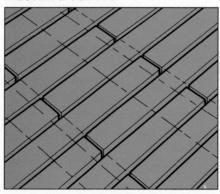

Place joints between pieces of decking over joists so that both ends can be nailed down. Stagger joints across neighboring joists.

JOIST SPLICES

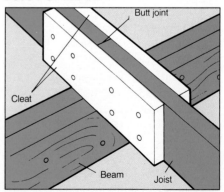

Butt ends of joists together over a beam, and nail or bolt cleats of the same-sized material to both sides of the splice.

and the most common sizes are 2 × 6, 2 × 8, and 2 × 10.

Joists are attached to beams or a ledger by nails or metal connectors (see page 94). Joists can be cantilevered out beyond each supporting beam for a distance of one-quarter of the span. This flexibility lets you derive maximum use of the material and gives you greater design flexibility. For example, joists spanning 10 feet from support to support can be as long as 15 feet overall (one-quarter of the 10-foot span is 2½ feet, so this much extension can be made at both ends of the joist). Such extensions can be made without increasing the size of the joists or the spacing. In any case, it is a good idea to insert cross bracing between the joists, to increase the overall stiffness of the joist and deck assembly. Some local codes require the use of crossbracing or bridging.

Beams. The beams are the heavier structural elements that support the joists. The size of the beam required depends on beam spacing and the spacing of the beam supports, that is, the posts and footings. In general, the trade-off between beam thickness and the number of supports is as follows: It is less expensive and time-consuming to have a thicker beam than it is to have more posts and footings. Often, beams are constructed by bolting or nailing together the same materials used for joists, which are smaller or thinner, to make the necessary larger size. This form of built-up beam is a standard construction technique. Beams are fastened to the posts or footings by metal connectors or cleats. These are available at most lumberyards or home supply stores. Beams can be cantilevered out from the posts to create an overhang. The same limit applies as for the joists—no more than one-quarter span beyond an end support.

Ledgers. If the deck is attached to the side of a house or other building, then the framing construction uses the existing building as one support. A ledger strip attached to the house supports the joists that are attached to it. Usually a ledger is a 2-inch-thick piece of wood (occasionally a steel beam is used) that is attached to the house by bolts, nails, or metal connectors. An-

BEAM SPLICES

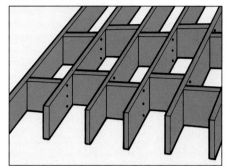

Butt ends of beams together on top of a post and bolt cleats of 1x material of the same width to both sides of the splice.

METHODS OF FASTENING JOISTS TO BEAMS

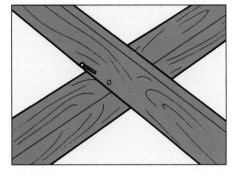

Toenailing joists to the tops of beams makes a weak connection and is not recommended.

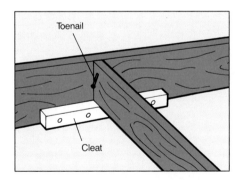

A joist end, resting on a wood cleat, can be nailed to the inside of a beam.

JOIST BLOCKING

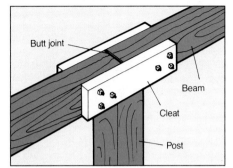

Insert blocking, made of the same-sized material, between the joists every 6 to 8 feet. Nail blocking in place from the other side.

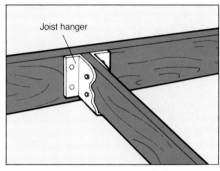

Ends of joists hanging inside beams are secured by metal joist hangers, nailed to both members.

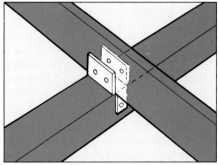

A joist can be secured to the top of a beam with a metal saddle anchor.

PARTS OF A LEDGER BEAM

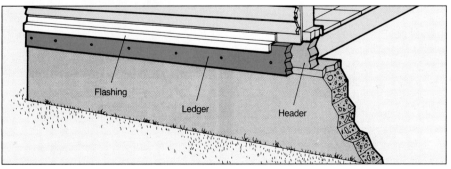

A wood ledger beam is bolted to the header joist (in a wood house), and a sheet of metal flashing is installed along the top edge to protect the ledger from moisture and decay.

other way to attach the joists is by using a metal angle strip, normally 3 inches × 3 inches. This is attached to the house with bolts or a similar device, and the joist ends rest on and are attached to the angle.

It is important to set the ledger strip so that the joists and the finished decking are at least 1 to 2 inches below the interior floor level. This will reduce the possibility of rain or snow entering the house. The minimum recommendation is to lower the decking 1 inch. If rain and snow conditions are unlikely or very infrequent in your area, the decking can be placed flush with the interior floor level.

Posts. The posts transfer the combined weight of the decking, joists, beams, and the user loads to the footings or the foundation. Most decks use 4 × 4 posts, but this size must be increased when posts support a structure higher than 6 feet above grade. A larger size is also required if the site slopes away from the house, or where heavy loads are expected. In addition, posts that have to support overhead cover or a roof must be larger than 4 × 4. Check your local building code for legal requirements and page 35 for recommendations.

Posts are connected to the footings or foundations either by being directly embedded in the concrete or by means of mechanical connectors. If your deck stands high off the ground, diagonal bracing is usually required to increase the stability of the deck. Cross bracing can be effectively integrated into the deck design by extending the pieces up to the height of the railing or by creating diagonal latticework around the base. Local building codes often dictate the bracing requirements.

Footings. The footings are the final destination of all the loads and forces supported by the decking, joists, beams, and posts. Local building codes are very specific about requirements for foundations. Ideally, footings should be constructed on undisturbed soil or on rock. If this is not possible, the soil should be compacted by tamping, using a mechanized or hand tamper. The footings must extend below the frost line, which varies in different parts of the country from a minimum depth of

METHODS OF ATTACHING LEDGERS TO WALLS

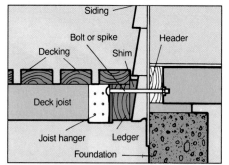

A ledger is bolted to the header joist of a wood house, using a shim if necessary.

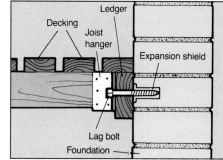

A ledger is fastened to masonry construction with an anchor bolt or an expansion bolt.

WAYS TO ATTACH BEAMS TO POSTS

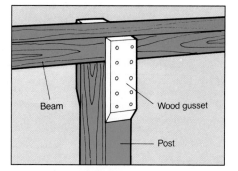
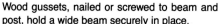

A metal saddle anchor, nailed to both beam and post, provides the strongest construction.

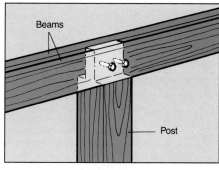

A beam can be attached with a metal strap nailed in place. Do not place a joist on the strap.

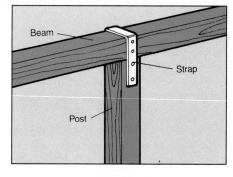

Wood gussets, nailed or screwed to beam and post, hold a wide beam securely in place.

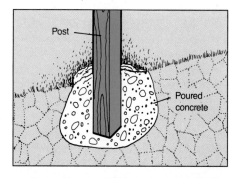

A double beam, made of two thinner pieces, sits in notches cut in the post top, held by bolts.

FOOTINGS FOR POSTS

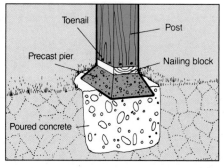

A precast concrete footing sits on a poured concrete foundation; the post is nailed to the nailing block.

A post may be embedded in a poured concrete foundation that is mounded up above the surface to shed water.

24 inches to a maximum of 48 inches. Local conditions may require special procedures; consult your building department.

Footings are usually made of poured-in-place concrete. They can be rectangular, circular, or square, depending on the connection and framework you've chosen. Footings should extend at least 2 to 6 inches out of the ground so that the post does not come in contact with the soil. This also lets rain drain rapidly away from the post and its point of contact with the footing. Where the posts are embedded in concrete rather than attached with metal connectors, the posts must be treated to prevent rot and insect damage. Old telephone poles make excellent posts for embedding in concrete. For low-level decks, concrete blocks or precast footings can be placed on compacted soil. However, this method does not guarantee that settlement will not occur.

Railings. Although railings are often considered decorative parts of a deck, building codes frequently dictate that they not only must be provided, but that they must measure a specified height. Railings can be attached to the decking or to the extended posts. Railings must be both stable and able to support a heavy load. People lean against them and furniture pushes against them. For this reason, the best design ties the railings in with the posts or beams (see Chapter 7).

OTHER BASIC CONSIDERATIONS

The position and design of the deck with regard to the house were discussed in Chapter 1. The deck location is influenced by specific building and legal requirements, and in turn influences the choice of materials and the estimate of quantities needed. The position of the deck in relation to the ground level is also of basic importance. This too is discussed in Chapter 1.

A COMBINED DECK AND ROOF STRUCTURE

To determine the specific requirements for a cover that will be built over a deck, you must first determine whether the

FOOTINGS FOR POSTS (CONTINUED)

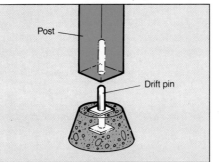

A metal drift pin, embedded in a precast concrete footing, holds the post in place.

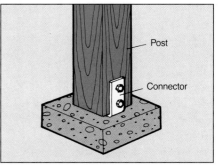

A metal connector, embedded in the concrete footing, is bolted to the bottom of the post.

WAYS TO ATTACH RAILINGS TO DECKS

Vertical elements of railings can be bolted to the outside joist.

The posts that support the deck can be extended up to provide support for railings.

METHOD FOR EXTENDING A DECK OVER A SLOPE

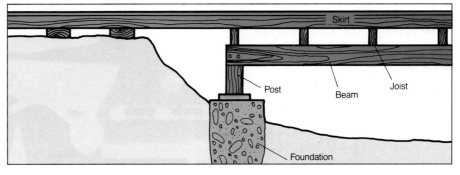

A deck may be built over sloping ground by using normal construction techniques to support the higher section (right) and resting the remainder of the deck directly on the ground.

DESIGN FOR COMBINING A DECK AND A COVER

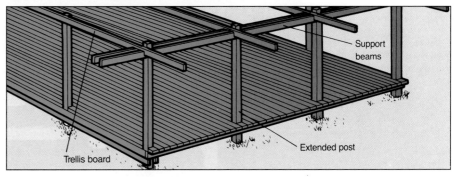

If you intend to provide cover for a deck, design it so that the posts that support the deck extend up to support the framework of the cover.

roof structure will be supported by the deck posts or by additional supports within the deck area. In both cases it is important that the roof structure be built first. In the case of a roof structure that is supported by existing walls or by spans from house to garage, the roof structure need not be built before the deck.

Constructing an overhead cover or roof structure for a deck is discussed in Chapter 10. If you plan to have your deck located under and supporting the roof structure, then the roof posts are extensions of the deck posts. The beams will be attached to the posts as they would in the construction of a deck without a roof structure (see Method 2, page 88). In this case, the decking will be placed around and fitted to the roof support posts, which extend up through the decking. No other modifications are necessary.

In case the roof structure is supported outside the deck area, it is a good idea to build the roof first, in order to eliminate any conflict between the construction of the roof and the deck. If there are no supports outside the deck area, the size of your roof may be limited. In this case, you might be able to build overhead coverage for only part of the deck rather than the entire area. If necessary, roof support posts can rest directly on an on-grade deck, as illustrated in Chapter 10.

BUILDING PERMITS
Before you begin actual construction of your deck (as discussed step by step in Chapter 5), be sure to obtain the necessary building permits from the local building department (see page 21). Most communities have a standard form to be filled out; they require copies of your proposed design. Once you have submitted the form and the drawings, along with the fee, a building inspector will review your proposed construction. Any changes required by local codes will be indicated. When all is approved, you will receive a building permit for a specified construction period. The duration is different in various locales. You must complete the construction within that period, although if you need more time to finish the work you can apply for an exten-

sion, which is usually granted.

During the work period, an inspector may examine the parts of the deck that are in place. Normally, the inspector will examine the foundation before it is covered over and conduct a final inspection before issuing an occupancy permit. This procedure varies from one community to another, so it is very important that you check your local requirements.

TOOLS FOR DECK BUILDING
You can build a deck with a modest set of tools.

For preparing the site you'll need a shovel and pick.

For mixing concrete you'll need a wheelbarrow, hoe, and shovel; if you

have a lot of footings to set, consider renting a canister-type cement mixer.

For setting out the plan, have a tape measure, ruler, twine, pencil, plumb bob, level, and framing square.

To cut wood you'll need a power circular saw, hand saw, and power jig saw.

For assembling the parts, a power drill, hammer, screwdriver, wrenches for bolts and lag screws, nail set, and chisel are necessary.

When finishing the surface, brushes, a pan, and a roller will be sufficient.

Be sure you have the proper safety equipment: goggles and gloves.

FASTENERS AND CONNECTORS
All the structural elements of a deck

EQUIPMENT FOR DECK CONSTRUCTION AND MAINTENANCE

The tools and equipment shown above are essential for preparing the site, cutting and assembling the parts, and maintaining the decks described in this book.

discussed at the beginning of this chapter—from the decking down through the posts—are fastened together by nails, screws, bolts, and metal connectors. Although it is possible to build a deck using only nails, screws, and bolts, you will have a more stable and longer-lasting deck if you use metal connectors, especially for joining posts, joists, ledgers, and other large structural members. The added cost is worth it in the long run. All fasteners and connectors that you use should be specifically intended for outdoor use, and must be rust-resistant.

NAILS

Use galvanized nails; they are available everywhere and will not rust as long as the zinc coating is not broken. They can be used for all parts of your deck construction. There are two other types of nails that resist rust. Aluminum nails resist rust better than galvanized nails, but they are not as strong and cost more. Stainless steel nails are available in some places; they resist rust best of all but are expensive.

Nails are usually sold by the pound, either from open stock or in packages. The price depends on their material and coating, if any, the design, and the size. The chart on page 160 gives information about nail sizes, the number of nails in a pound, and standard designations, shown in penny sizes: 10d means ten-penny (the *d* denotes the old English *pennyweight*).

There are two important rules of thumb to remember. First, always use nails that are about twice as long as the thickness of the top piece of lumber you are nailing. For example, if you are putting down 2 × 4 decking, use 12- or 16-penny nails (the 2 × 4 is 1½ inches thick; the nails are 3¼ and 3½ inches long). Second, blunt the sharp points of nails with a hammer to prevent the nails from splitting the wood.

TYPES OF NAILS

Nails used in deck construction are shown at the right; the most common types are described below.

Common nails and *box nails* are used to secure decking and other structural members. They have large, flat heads.

BASIC PROCEDURES FOR USING FASTENERS

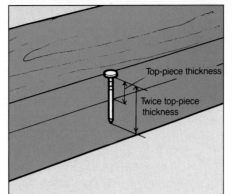

Nail thin pieces to thick pieces, using nails that are twice the width of the thin pieces.

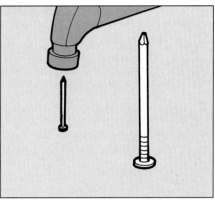

Blunt the ends of sharp nails with a hammer, to avoid splitting lumber. Drill pilot holes near the ends of lumber pieces.

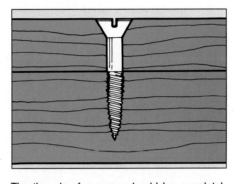

The threads of a screw should be completely sunk into the second piece of wood. The head should be countersunk below the surface.

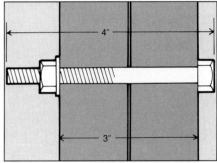

Use bolts that are one inch longer than the total thickness of the boards being joined together.

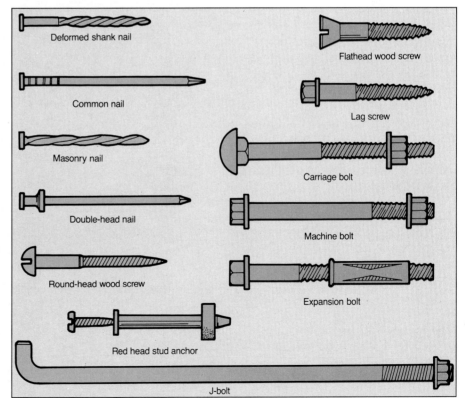

Each connector shown here has its individual function in deck construction; when used for that purpose (described in the text), it ensures a safe, reliable structure.

Finishing nails are used when an exposed nail head is undesirable. These small-headed nails are used on parts such as railings and seats.

Spiral nails are used for plywood, roof coverings, and sometimes for decking lumber. These nails hold very well.

Double-head nails have two heads so that they can be removed from temporary construction such as braces and forms.

Special-purpose nails such as *concrete nails*, *joist-hanger nails*, and *fiberglass panel nails* are made for the limited uses indicated by their names.

SCREWS AND BOLTS
These fasteners are more expensive than nails and take longer to install but the resulting connection is stronger. They are recommended for railings, stairs, benches, and other constructions that must resist a great deal of pressure against the connection.

USING SCREWS
The threaded part of the screw should reach completely into the second piece of wood. First drill a hole through the top piece of wood the same size and depth as the threadless part of the screw (called the shank), and then drill a matching, smaller-diameter pilot hole in the lower piece. This removes enough bulk to prevent splitting, but leaves plenty of wood for the threads to bite into. A screw-pilot bit in a power drill produces both size holes quickly while the two pieces of wood are held in alignment. It also makes a shallow countersink hole for the screw head.

USING BOLTS
Buy bolts that are one inch longer than the combined thickness of the pieces being joined. Drill a hole through the wood that is 1/16 inch larger than the bolt diameter.

METAL CONNECTORS
When used in conjunction with screws and nails, metal connectors add rigidity to a deck and ensure a stronger and longer-lasting connection. They are available in preformed shapes intended for making specific joints, such as post to footing and joist to ledger. The most useful types are shown below. Use joist-hanger nails to make all the connections.

DECK FINISHES
It is a good idea to apply some sort of finish to the exposed wood surfaces of your deck to protect it from the effects of weather and sun. If you want to see the grain, texture, and/or color of the wood, use a water-repellent, natural finish containing a wood preservative. There are three types of deck finishes:

Clear, natural finish delays the effects of weathering but allows grain, texture, and color to remain visible.

Semitransparent finish is easy to apply. It lets the grain and texture of the wood show but modifies the color. This might be useful, for example, if you want the deck to match the house.

Solid-color stain lets the wood texture show but masks the grain and the original color. Applied to badly weathered wood, a solid-color stain produces a durable, renewed finish.

These natural finishes are penetrating compounds that enter the wood but do not leave a surface film. A surface coating will break and deteriorate in time, hastening wood decay.

If you want to cover the grain, texture, and color of the wood entirely, apply paint. Use an exterior oil-base or an exterior latex paint. A latex paint goes on easier than an oil-base paint; brushes, rollers, pans, and hands are easily cleaned in water. Oil-base paint provides stronger, longer-lasting protection, especially on weathered, rough, or previously painted wood, but turpentine or paint thinner is required for cleanup.

METAL CONNECTORS FOR DECK CONSTRUCTION

Use metal connectors and plates designed specifically for joining deck components; they provide the most stable and long-lasting decks.

(Above) Well-chosen woods unite the house and deck with a dramatic shade tree at one end.

(Right) This deck features an open-air kitchen at one corner. Counter, cabinets, and box planters all have the same wood-and-tile motif in their design.

(Above) Low, broad benches line the edges of a corner deck. The flooring is laid flush to the structural beams.

(Right) These platforms laid directly on the ground are easy to construct. They provide areas for seating and for displaying colorful flowering plants.

Decks can flow around and encompass such man-made features as this soaking pool beside a lagoon, or such striking natural features as these rock formations.

This three-level deck provides for a variety of activities and offers a fine view of the surroundings. Boxed steps lead from the ground to a first level that features built-in saplings and low benches. The middle level provides a dining area accessible from the house, and connects to a sundeck on the third level.

A multilevel deck can provide effective terracing. It is easier to construct and maintain, and offers more useful area, than terraced soil.

Choose deck materials with an eye to how they will look after weathering. Undeniably handsome when brand new, this redwood deck developed a pleasing, far more natural appearance in the course of ten years' exposure to the elements.

Decking in poolside areas is easy to clean and drains away surface water immediately. Any shape pool can be accommodated, and the deck area can be as large or small as desired.

A raised deck solves the problem of a pool structure that extends above ground level; it can also hide pumps, filters, and other pool equipment.

Latticework made of lath provides shade but permits air circulation over the raised portion of this deck. The pattern is repeated in the railing fill-in.

(Left) Low continuous steps that require no railing give this deck an open feeling.

(Below) Planters help unite this deck with lush surrounding plants. The diagonal decking pattern is both visually interesting and appropriate to the angled shape.

(Opposite) The split design and raised center of this overhead covering are not only striking, but provide increased air circulation. The roof boards are mounted on edge to provide maximum shade from angled sunlight.

(Above) A lattice fence provides privacy but does not totally wall in the space.

(Left) This canvas covering is both colorful and adjustable for various weather conditions; construction is described in Chapter 10.

A major deck area is integrated into the design of this modern home. A pool hidden from view on the main approach level can be seen from the deck. Glass panels in the railing provide wind protection without obstructing vision. On the lake side of the house, a sundeck connects with a spa on a lower level. The railing construction is different, but the curved walls carry through the distinctive exterior design.

(Right) Hanging and boxed planters, and an open-frame roof between two side walls, turn this deck area into a conservatory garden.

(Below) Dense, mature trees and bushes give privacy to this open deck.

Harmony with its surroundings is the key to this deck's success. Special features include the open-work roof over the circular brick-paved area, and lighting concealed among the plants.

(Above) The railing around this deck is also a back for a continuous bench. The design incorporates existing trees for shade and hammock support.

(Opposite) The wood siding of the house is matched in the decking and in the surrounding low walls. These function as railing, bench, and planter areas. Small lights atop the walls mark the perimeter and the steps at night.

A sensitive combination of materials and design gives this decked-in corner a totally natural feeling. The decking on the steps overhangs support timbers used as risers.

Latticework provides screening and air circulation both above and below this deck. A view from above reveals the openwork roof construction, built-in benches, and a step-down level that is accented by a change of direction in the decking pattern.

An extended attached deck corresponds to different floor levels in this double-gable house. The lower-level balcony deck is connected by full-width steps to the broader upper level. Stairs to the ground from both levels have full risers and sturdy railings.

Steps determine access and flow.
These broad, shallow-rise steps
provide easy movement and a
graceful visual transition between
related levels.

(Right) A major change of level requires full-fledged stairs and a substantial railing.

(Below left) A change of pathway direction should be made on one platform level.

(Below right) Recessed risers make these broad steps seem to float above one another.

This deck extends the interior floor level to a broad outdoor area. It is accessible from two different parts of the house and provides access to the flagstone-paved area surrounding the pool.

A gazebo is given privacy by surrounding foliage at one end of this long deck. A sweeping curve increases the deck area significantly.

Decking covers the earth around a pool, where a low wall, picket fences, and trees enclose the area. The deck is raised one step from the umbrella table area, and its diagonally laid decking extends slightly over the edge of the pool. Wooden flower boxes, a colorful accent, can easily be moved for deck maintenance.

This raised attached deck has a lower level with a private spa corner. The spa is flanked on two sides by a railing bench. Features of this deck include a flowerbox wall along steps on one side, a boxed tree and below-railing-level light fixtures, and cantilevered bench construction for post-free corners.

(Next page) A thick-thin design rhythm in the railing of this deck is echoed in the wide and narrow boards of the decking. In the unusual roof construction, spaced strips are attached below their supporting members.

5 CONSTRUCTING A DECK

This chapter describes the construction of a deck in step-by-step detail. Although one person's level of craftsmanship and assembly skills varies from that of another, the information and techniques described here are fundamental to all skill levels. Furthermore, the construction process is simplified so that the time necessary for construction is kept to a minimum.

To make this chapter as informative and uncomplicated as possible, the sequence of events described applies to a basic deck design. You can adjust these instructions to accommodate the variations of your own design. Every attempt has been made to simplify the individual steps so that you can see the similarities and differences between design choices. There may be parts of the construction procedure that you will want to contract out; for example, you might want to have a contractor make the concrete footings, especially if your plan calls for a great many of them. If you follow this procedure, simply pick up where the contractor has left off. The purpose here is to provide you with many of the construction tips that professionals use in building a deck.

This chapter deals with building a simple, freestanding wood deck that is supported on posts and concrete footings. The following chapter explains

A BASIC DESIGN FOR A WOOD DECK

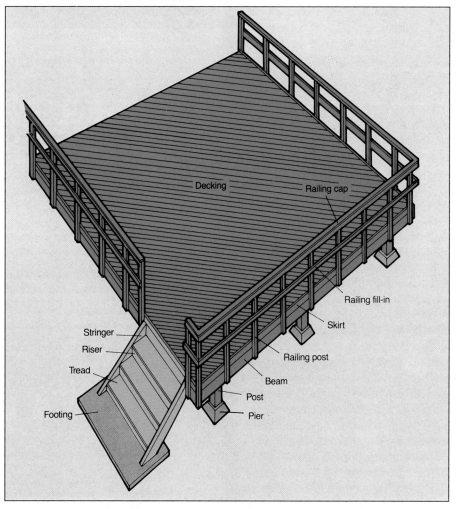

A standard wood deck with stairs and railing uses the structural elements identified above.

how to attach a deck to a house by means of a ledger, how to build a raised deck that requires post bracing, and how to make a simple parquet deck that is laid directly on a prepared grade.

STEP 1
PREPARING THE SITE

Before you order the building materials, clear the working area. Remove all shrubs, rocks, and other obstacles that are not part of your design. Remove all wood (which attracts termites). Strip away grass and other ground cover.

Make sure the ground slopes away from the deck to ensure proper drainage. Build up the soil at one side of the deck or in the center if necessary, and slope it away from the high point to make positive drainage. Standing water can develop dank odors as well as provide a breeding place for insects. A slope of ⅛ inch per foot is enough to prevent accumulation.

If any roof gutters empty into or near the deck area, angle the downspouts to direct the runoff away from the deck. If that is not practical, install an underground line to drain water away from the deck to a dry well in a lower area. Check local codes for dry-well restrictions. Dig a 1½-foot-deep trench that slopes from the downspout outlet down to the well, which should be about 2 feet wide and 2 or 3 feet deep. Fill the well with small stones. Run a line of 4-inch-diameter drainage tile in the trench, from outlet to well; cover the tile joints with roofing felt and 8 to 10 inches of gravel. Top the trench and dry well with a layer of dirt. The fill will settle over time, so pile it a few inches above the adjoining ground level.

STEP 2
STAKING OUT THE DECK

Start by laying out the deck on the ground. Even a freestanding deck should be built parallel or at right angles to a nearby house. Choose one corner of the deck near the house, a wall face or other structure, and mark it by driving a stake into the cleared, evenly-sloping ground. Stake out the four corners of the deck, using the triangulation survey method described on page 83 to make all dimensions exact and all corners square.

PREPARING THE SITE

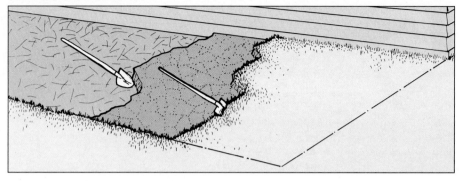

To prepare the site for deck building, remove all grass, plants, roots, and wood. Work the bare ground with spade and rake so that it slopes away from the house and the deck.

DECK SITE DRAINAGE

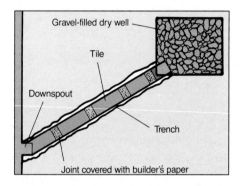

Make the ground under the deck slope away at least ⅛″ per foot to provide positive drainage.

Plan view: If site slope does not provide enough drainage from a downspout, make a dry well.

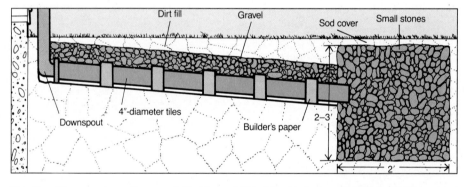

Elevation: Place the dry well, a gravel-filled hole of 15 to 20 cubic feet, away from the deck area and lead excessive runoff from a downspout to the well through a sloping run of tile.

STAKING OUT THE DECK

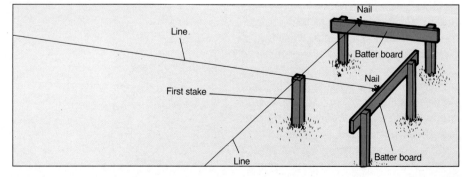

Batter boards set at right angles to each other provide support for lines that mark the sides of the proposed deck. A stake at the intersection marks a point of measurement.

MEASURING BY THE TRIANGULATION METHOD

Set up two batter boards, as shown here, about 1 foot outside the first stake. Drive a nail into the board that is at right angles to the structure to which you are orienting the deck, and from that nail run a line parallel to the structure across the stake. Measure the desired dimension of the deck along that line and drive another stake. Set up batter boards in the same way at that location.

Now, measure along the line 3 feet from the first stake A, and drive another stake B. From the first stake A run a second line perpendicular to the first. Measure out 4 feet to locate point C. If this second line is exactly at a right angle to the first, the diagonal between the 4-foot point C and the 3-foot point B will be exactly 5 feet, and you have a right-angle triangle. If it is not 5 feet, move the point C left or right until the diagonal measures 5 feet, and stake that point.

Stretch a line from stake A straight across C and fasten it to a temporary stake outside the intended deck area. Measure along this line from A and mark off the deck dimension in that direction. Drive a stake there and set up batter boards. Then use the 3-4-5 triangulation method to extend another line at right angles to the A–C line (it will run parallel to your first, A–B line). Measure off to the next corner, stake it, and continue until you have all four corners of the deck area connected by right-angle lines.

The 3-4-5 method is good for small distances. For greater accuracy with deck dimensions longer than 8 feet, use multiples of 3-4-5 to lay out right angles: 9-12-15 or 12-16-20, or more. Batter boards can also be used to lay out other angles.

Make sure that your batter boards are firmly in the ground, and the lines securely fastened to nails, or your dimensions will be off. Incorrect dimensions can cause problems later when you assemble the lumber pieces.

Check the accuracy of a square or rectangular deck layout by measuring the diagonals between opposite corners. If they are equal, all corners are right angles.

STAKING OUT RIGHT-ANGLE CORNERS

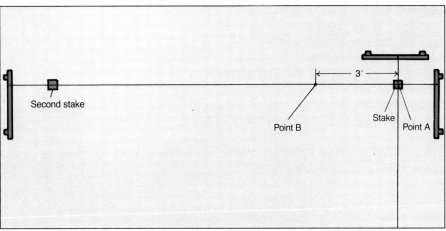

1. Run a line across two stakes, representing one side of the deck. Measure from point A on the first stake along this line 3 feet and mark point B.

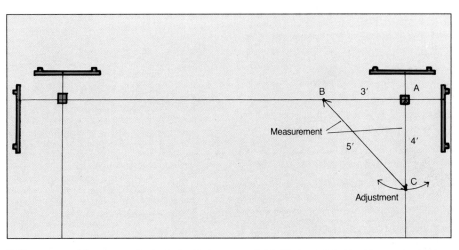

2. Run a second line perpendicular to the first across point A. Mark point C, 4 feet from point A. Move line AC so that the distance BC is exactly 5 feet. Angle BAC is now a 90° angle.

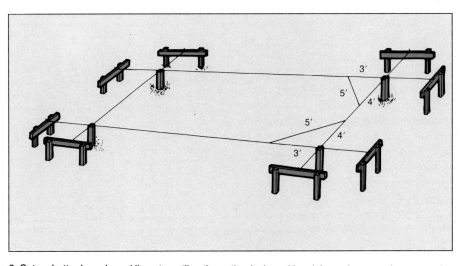

3. Set up batter boards and lines to outline the entire deck, making right angles at each corner using the 3-4-5 triangle method described above.

STEP 3
LAYING OUT FOOTING HOLES

Once you have located all the deck corners, you can stake out the locations for the footings. Since the strings mark the outside dimensions of the deck, refer to your deck plans to see whether the posts are at the edge of the deck or set back 18 to 24 inches from the edge.

If the outside edges of the joists, beams, and posts are to be in line, the point where the strings intersect marks the outside corner of the post. Use a plumb line to find this spot on the ground beneath the intersecting strings. Drive a stake into the ground inside this spot to mark the post center, until it is time to dig the hole.

If the outside posts are set back from the deck perimeter, set up lines parallel to the perimeter lines and locate the post positions with a ruler, plumb bob, and stake. To find the positions of other posts inside the perimeter, use the techniques described above.

STEP 4
MAKING THE FOOTINGS

A deck footing is basically a hole in the ground filled with concrete to which the deck posts are attached. It is best to mount the posts on concrete at least 6 inches above grade to prevent wood decay. The type of footing you choose dictates the size and depth of the hole to be dug. The most effective footing for your design depends on the nature of your soil. If it is stable, just dig a hole $12 \times 12 \times 8$ inches, fill it with concrete built up to a slight mound, then insert a metal connector (see page 48).

If the soil is soft clay or a similar spongy material, use a mass-form concrete footing. This is an oversize hole filled with concrete and capped with a wood form that extends the concrete about 6 inches above grade. An anchor strap is set into the concrete. If the soil is very loose, you may have to dig down to find a stable surface on which to build the deck. If conditions are still not good, rent a power compactor to make the desired surface.

On stable soil you can dig a shallow hole, set in a precast concrete pier, then fill in around the pier with fresh concrete. Precast piers usually have a

FINDING FOOTING LOCATIONS

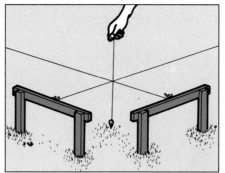

If the intersection of the lines marks the center of the deck post, drop a plumb line from that point and mark the ground.

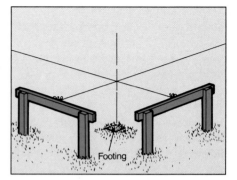

Dig a hole beneath the guide lines with a post hole digger or spade, and install the footing, using one of the types shown below.

TYPES OF DECK FOOTINGS

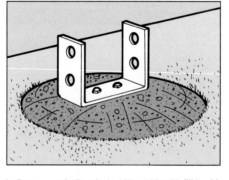

In firm ground, dig a hole 12″ × 12″ × 8″, fill it with concrete, and insert a metal post connector. Be sure the connector is vertical.

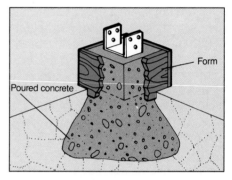

In softer ground, dig a larger hole and set a wood form over it so that 5 or 6 inches of concrete sits above ground level.

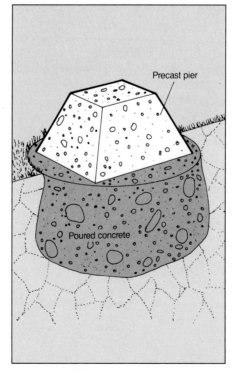

You can combine concrete poured into a hole with a precast concrete pier set on top of the fresh concrete; be sure the pier is level.

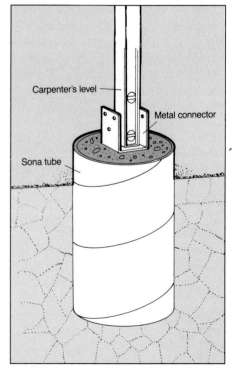

A Sona tube is a ready-made form for poured concrete. If you install a metal connector in fresh concrete, be sure it sits level.

wood nailing block on top, or a metal connector, such as a drift pin, for attaching the post to the pier.

Another method of making footings is especially useful in sandy or gravelly soils. It uses the Sona Tube, a cylindrical waxed-cardboard form that keeps the surrounding soil from falling into the space where the concrete is to be poured; it is available in a range of sizes. The Sona Tube is cut off a little above the desired level of concrete and placed in the post hole, which is dug somewhat oversize. Fill soil is then compacted around it to make sure that it is stable and will not shift. The tube is braced using 2 × 4s fastened to the top.

There are two ways to set the posts with Sona Tubes. The preferred method is to fill the tube with concrete up to a few inches above grade, smooth it off, and insert a post strap or other metal connector into the concrete at the right level. Use a carpenter's level to make sure the connector is vertical.

Another way to use the tubes (if it is allowed by local codes) is to insert the post itself in a larger diameter tube and then pour concrete around the post, making sure it is plumb and aligned with all other posts. Brace the post with 2 × 4s set into the ground and aligned in two directions to make a right angle.

Other brands of tubes may be cut lengthwise before use and tied with wire or twine to make removal easy. If the inside of the tube is not treated to prevent concrete sticking, smear a little motor oil on the inner surface.

A minimum tube diameter of 12 inches is recommended for 4 × 4 posts placed on top of the footing. Where a 4 × 4 post is embedded in the tube, a minimum 16-inch tube diameter is recommended.

In northern climates where severe freezing occurs, the cement in the Sona Tube may crack unless it is reinforced with a steel rod. Insert a No. 5 size steel reinforcing rod in the tube, just short of the desired height.

Another technique for making footings is to dig a hole larger than a masonry block and about 6 inches deep. Fill this hole with concrete and place a masonry block on top. Fill the open spaces in the block with concrete and

TYPES OF DECK FOOTINGS (CONTINUED)

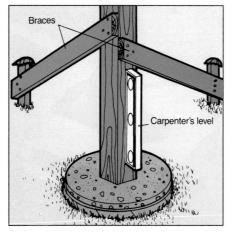

You can place the deck post directly in the fresh concrete in the Sona tube. Brace the post and use a level to make sure it's perpendicular.

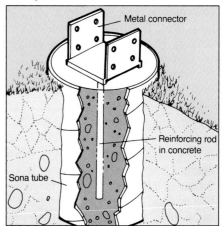

In cold climates, add a reinforcing rod to concrete in a Sona tube. Install a metal connector to support the post.

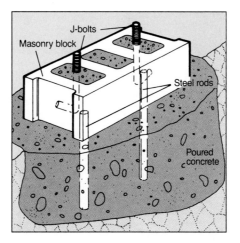

Masonry blocks make good post footings; set them on masses of poured concrete and drive rods through the blocks into the concrete.

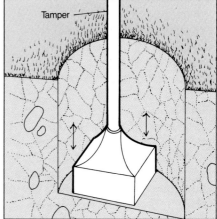

If the ground beneath your proposed footing is loose, compact it with a hand tamper. Rent a mechanical tamper for larger areas.

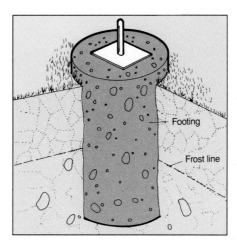

For adequate deck support, your footing should extend below the frost line. Check your local building code for specific information.

GROUND COVERING

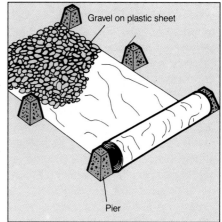

After footings and piers are in place, cover the ground under the proposed deck with a black plastic sheet and spread gravel over the sheet.

level it. Drive pieces of reinforcing rod through the block into the concrete below. Insert J-bolts or other metal connectors into the block holes for post attachment.

In areas with severe freezing, codes may specify that footings must be placed below frost level, to avoid heaving that could damage the deck.

After all the footings have been poured and the connectors put in place, wait three days and then remove the bracing, forms, and cardboard from the concrete. When the footings have been stripped and the ground compacted to level, put down a 4- or 6-mil-thick sheet of polyethylene over the ground that will be under the deck, and cover the sheet with 2 to 4 inches of small gravel. This creates a maintenance-free area.

MIXING AND POURING CONCRETE

Your decision whether to mix your own concrete or to have it delivered by truck, ready to pour, depends on how many footings you need and whether you would rather spend time and effort on mixing or money on premixed concrete. To make a few footings, the simplest method is to buy sacks of dry mix. One 90-pound sack will make ⅔ cubic foot of concrete, which equals one 12 × 12 × 8-inch footing, the standard size. (A 12 × 12 × 6-inch footing equals ½ cubic foot, and a 12 × 12 × 12-inch footing equals 1 cubic foot.)

You can mix up 3 or 4 cubic feet of concrete in a wheelbarrow. Dump in the required amount of dry mix and mix it up thoroughly with a shovel or hoe. You will need about 4 gallons of water for 3 cubic feet and 5 gallons for 4 cubic feet. Scoop out a hollow in the middle of the dry mix and pour in about half of the water. Mix everything thoroughly. Add the remaining water a little at a time and mix constantly. Watch the consistency of the concrete carefully. Wet concrete should be stiff and easily formed into stable shapes, not sloshing around, nor dry and crumbly.

When a batch of concrete is ready, pour the footings immediately. If you are using precast piers or masonry blocks on top of fresh concrete, put them in place immediately and align

MIXING CONCRETE

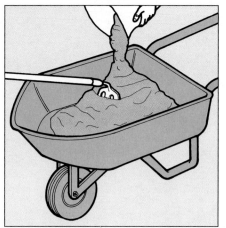

1. Small amounts of concrete are easily made in a wheelbarrow. Empty sacks of dry mix into the barrow and mix everything thoroughly with a hoe.

2. When the dry materials are completely mixed, make a hollow in the center of the pile to receive the water.

3. Pour about half the required water into the hollow and mix everything thoroughly. Don't let any dry material accumulate.

4. Test the consistency of the concrete as you go; it should mound up easily into a stable cone. Don't add more water than is needed.

PRESERVING POST ENDS FROM ROT

It's a good idea to soak all newly cut post ends in a barrel of wood preservative solution overnight.

In damp areas, use a post-to-footing connector that raises the post an inch or so off the footing. This allows the post end to dry.

them. Insert any metal connectors into the concrete at once, and make sure they are level and properly aligned.

Before you decide to use premixed concrete, make a rough estimate of the amount you will need. Do not forget to include stair footings. Premixed concrete is usually sold by the cubic yard, which is 27 cubic feet. Call your supplier to find out what quantity he will deliver and at what price. Be ready to pour the footings when the truck pulls up; have a wheelbarrow handy.

STEP 5
ATTACHING POSTS TO FOOTINGS

When the concrete footings, piers, and metal connectors have been installed, set up the posts. Use only pressure-treated lumber for posts, and for now cut them about 6 inches longer than their finished height. Later you can cut them down individually to accommodate differences in footing height once you've chosen one of the beam-attaching methods, explained below. Each post must be set plumb on its footing.

All the hardware you use to attach the posts to footings or piers should be high quality, galvanized materials. The fasteners must anchor the post securely to the footing or pier. This is crucial in windy areas, for decks high off the ground, and for decks that support heavy weight. If you live in a wet climate, use a metal connector that raises the post end off the footing; this lets the post dry out, preventing decay.

A common way of connecting a post to a pier is to toenail the bottom of the post to a wood nailing block set in the pier. This is a weak method and is not recommended. If the nails rust out, the post could "walk" off the pier.

Set up the posts in the connectors. Use two 2 × 4s set at a right angle to hold the posts vertical; check the posts twice to make sure they are both perpendicular and square to the lines of the beams they will support.

STEP 6
SETTING UP THE BEAMS

There are two ways to attach beams to posts. In Method 1, the beams are attached to and rest on the tops of the posts. In Method 2, the beams are at-

ATTACHING BEAMS TO POST TOPS

1. If your design calls for attaching the beams to the post tops, use a metal beam-to-post connector for the most stable construction.

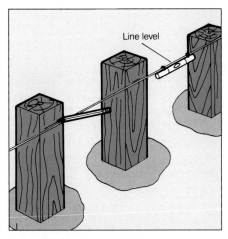

2. Establish the desired post height (see text) on the first post, and mark the other posts for cutting with a line and line level.

3. Cut the post tops off level with a circular saw. 4 × 4 or larger posts will require cuts on two or more sides.

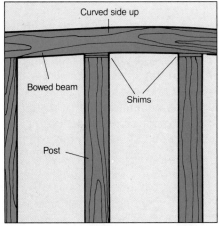

4. Lay the beams on top of the posts with the high sides up. Fill any gaps with shims. Install metal connectors on top of the shims.

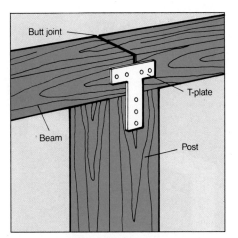

Splice beams with a butt joint only on top of a post. Secure splice with a T-plate on each side. Additional connectors are not needed.

5. Cut off the ends of the beams according to your plans. Length of overhang may be specified by local building codes.

tached to the sides of the posts; the tops of the beams and the tops of the posts are flush. These two methods are described in detail below.

METHOD 1
BEAMS ON POST TOPS

If your design calls for the beams to rest on the post tops, calculate the post height this way: Establish the deck height above grade, subtract the thickness of the decking, the depth of the joist if the joist sits on top of the beams, and the depth of the beam.

Mark the calculated height on a corner post as a reference point. From this point run a string line with a line level (or a straight 2 × 4 with a carpenter's level) out to the other posts and mark the heights. Cut off the post tops, making sure each cut is level.

Lay the beams across the tops of the posts, according to your plan. Look along each beam to see if it bows up or down; if it does, turn the high side up. Check to see that each beam is level. If it is not, slip thin pieces of wood between beam and post to raise the low spots. Install the metal connector you have chosen. Toenailing the beam to the post is *not* recommended. The wood may split and the nails cannot resist beam twisting.

BEAM SPLICING

If the beams you are using do not span the full length of your deck, you may have to splice two shorter beams together. Center the joint over the top of a post as shown on page 87. Stagger multiple splices across the deck.

Now you can cut off the ends of the beams. Use a chalk line across the deck to make sure that all the ends will be cut off at the same point.

METHOD 2
BEAMS ATTACHED TO POST SIDES

If your plan calls for beams to be attached to the sides of the posts with lag screws, then the height of the posts is the height of the decking top minus the combined thickness of the decking and the joist depth, if the joists sit on the beam (see below).

Establish the desired decking height at one corner and calculate the height

ATTACHING BEAMS TO POST SIDES

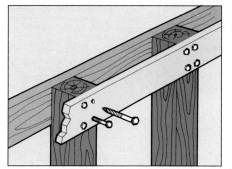

1. Beams may be attached to the sides of the posts with lag bolts.

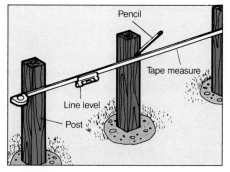

2. Determine the desired post height (see text) on the first post, and mark the other posts for cutting.

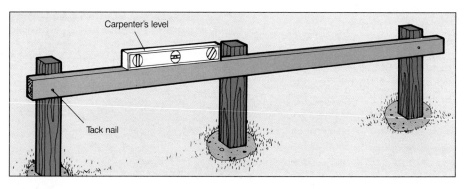

3. Tacknail a beam in place at the cutting marks and make certain it is level. Set up the other beams in the same way.

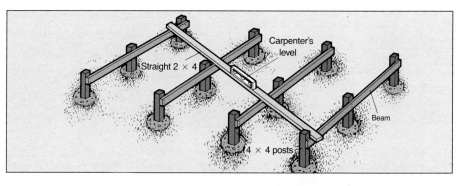

4. Check the level of all beams with a carpenter's level and a 2 × 4 laid diagonally across them. Repeat the check on the opposite diagonal.

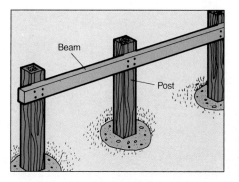

5. When all the beams are tacknailed in place and level, drill holes for the bolts and install them.

6. Cut the post tops off level with the beams, with a circular or straight saw.

of that post; mark it clearly on the post as a reference point. Tack-nail one beam to each post in its row. (Partially drive two or three nails to make a temporary connection.) Start at the corner reference point and make sure the beam is straight and level as you tack-nail. Attach the rest of the beams in the same way, leveling them to the first beam. Then lay a straight 2 × 4 and a level diagonally across the beams to check that everything is level.

Now attach the beams permanently to the posts with ¼ × 3 inch galvanized lag screws. Use at least two and preferably four at each connection. Drill holes as described on page 48. When all the beams are attached, cut the tops of the posts flush with the beams (unless the posts must extend up to support railings or roof structures). Cut off the ends of the beams, using a chalk line to make sure all the ends are aligned.

STEP 7
INSTALLING THE JOISTS

Once the beams have been attached to the posts, you are ready to install the joists. Two common methods are described below—setting the joists on top of the beams, and hanging the joists between the beams.

METHOD 1
JOISTS RESTING ON BEAMS

If the joists rest on top of the beams, it simplifies construction to build the skirt first. The skirt is composed of the outside joists that span across the ends of the beams, plus the joists that cap the ends of all the other joists.

First, carefully cut two skirt end joists to the design length. Then toenail them at the ends of the beams. Use two or three 16-penny galvanized nails for each connection. Now, measure the distance from one skirt joist to the opposite one; cut a cap joist to fit and install it. Do the same for the other cap joist. On the top edges of the cap joists, mark out the complete joist pattern on 24-inch centers. Measure carefully between the cap joists and cut inside joists to fit accurately.

Start installing the inside joists at one side of the deck and work across to the other side, toenailing both ends of the joists to the beams and nailing

INSTALLING JOISTS ON BEAM TOPS

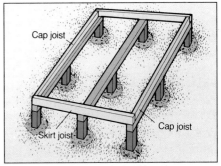

1. If your design calls for placing the joists on top of the beams, install the end or skirt joists first.

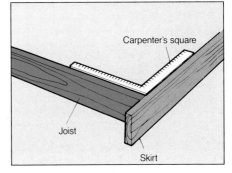

2. Install cap joists between the two skirt joists. All remaining joists fit between the caps.

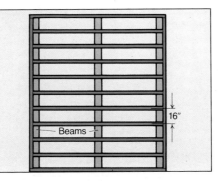

3. To support standard decking, install joists at regular intervals between the cap joists.

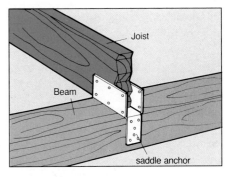

Use a carpenter's square to check that each joist is installed at right angles to the cap joists.

TYPES OF JOIST CONNECTIONS

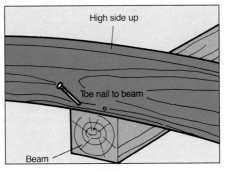

Joists inside a skirt can be toenailed to each beam and nailed through the cap joists.

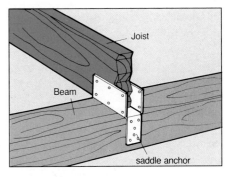

A metal saddle anchor makes a stronger connection. Nail to both joist and beam.

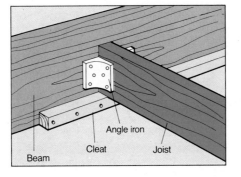

A joist can be connected to the side of a beam with angle irons. Rest the joist on a cleat.

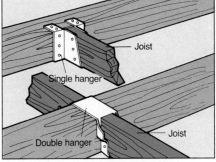

Metal joist hangers make the strongest connections for joists installed between beams.

through the face of the cap joists into the ends of inside joists. As you lay each joist up in position, sight across it to see if it is bowed; always turn the high side up. Toenail the joist to all inside beams. Use a framing square to make sure the joist is perpendicular to the beams. Do not be concerned if the last two joists have a little more or less than 24 inches between them.

Another way to attach the joists to the tops of the beams is with beam saddle anchors, metal connectors that are nailed to both joist and beam. Although it takes a little longer to install, a saddle anchor makes a stronger connection.

METHOD 2
JOISTS ATTACHED TO BEAM SIDES

If the joists hang down between the beams, you have a choice of connection methods. One is the combination cleat and angle iron connection. This requires cutting a wood cleat to size, then installing it with two metal pieces. The other metal connectors shown here are all one piece and can be attached more quickly. The double joist hanger is useful for attaching joists to inside beams; it lines up two joists automatically. For making connections to outside beams, you can use a single hanger (which also has a metal piece that sits on top of the beam), or one of the several anchor designs that are attached only to the side of the beam. Use 16-penny galvanized joist-hanger nails.

Whatever connector you use, start at one side of the deck and mark the joist location on the ends of the outside beams. If there are inside beams, snap a chalk line between the marks on the outside beams to mark the joist locations on the inside beams. Space the inside connectors so that the joists are 24 inches on center. Before you nail in a connector completely, use a framing square to check that both ends of the joist are exactly square to the beams.

JOIST SPLICING

If you cannot buy joists that extend the full length of your design, splice two pieces together. Measure carefully so that the splice will be centered on top of a beam, and if possible also centered

ATTACHING JOISTS TO BEAM SIDES

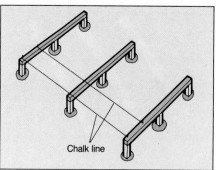

1. To hang joists between the beams, mark the position of each joist end using a chalk line.

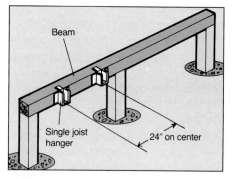

2. Install joist hangers, centering them on the marks made in Step 1. Use 10d or 12d nails.

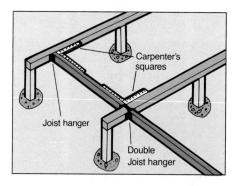

3. Make sure the joist ends are at right angles to the beams. Then nail the hangers to the joists.

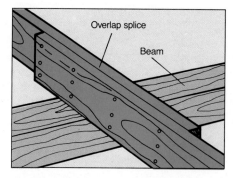

An overlap splice also must rest on a beam. Note that it puts the joist ends out of alignment.

JOIST SPLICING

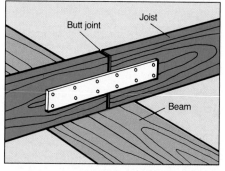

A butt joint splice must rest on top of a beam. Use two metal straps to secure the joint.

JOIST BLOCKING

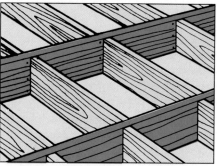

To strengthen long joists or support unusual decking patterns, nail blocking in place.

JOIST LAYOUT FOR DECKING VARIATIONS

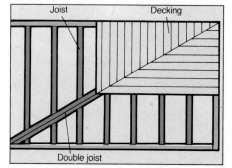

The ends of all decking must be nailed to a joist. Plan your installation to provide this support.

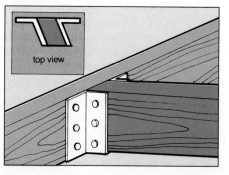

To support decking that runs at diagonals to the beams, secure joists with skewed hangers.

over a post. Do not place adjacent splices over the same beam; stagger them across the deck.

Two splices are shown on the opposite page. One is made by overlapping the ends of two joists. Cut the sections so that the ends extend over the beam at least 6 inches. If you are using 2 × 6 or 2 × 10 joists, drive 20-penny nails right through the splice and clinch the nail ends. You can also bolt or screw the two joist ends together.

Another way to splice joists is to butt them together and attach metal or wood cleats on both sides. The cleats should cover more than half the width of the splice. Offset the nailing pattern in opposite cleats.

BRACING AND BLOCKING

If your joists are more than 8 feet long, brace them to prevent twisting. Bracing also helps to stiffen the deck and to spread out the weight placed on it.

The standard method of strengthening joists is to install blocking—pieces of lumber the same size as the joists that are nailed at right angles between the joists. This method is used for joists up to 2 × 10 size. Stagger the blocks so that you can nail them easily from the other side of the joist. Install blocking at intervals of 6 to 8 feet for a normal design with long, parallel pieces of decking. For other patterns place the blocking so that it will support the ends of short pieces of decking.

If your joists are 2 × 10 or larger, wood or metal bridges are preferred. Both types use a pair of pieces in an X pattern. For wood bridges you must cut many small lengths of 1 × 4s or 2 × 4s, miter the ends, and toenail the pairs to the joists. Use at least two 6- or 7-penny nails at each connection. Although more expensive, metal bridges are easier and quicker to install.

BOXING A TREE

If you are building a deck that surrounds a tree or other obstruction, you need to strengthen the joist pattern at that point. Nail two pieces of joist lumber together to box the tree in one direction, and additional pieces to brace the box in the other direction. The box must support decking all around the tree. Leave space for growth.

JOIST BRIDGING

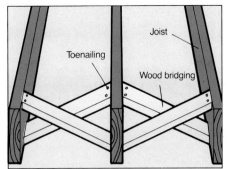

Long joists must have bridging to prevent twisting. Small braces of 1 × 4 or 2 × 4 can be cut to fit and nailed in place in a X pattern.

BOXING A TREE

1. If you build a deck around a tree, add additional joists to make a box like that shown above, to support all the decking.

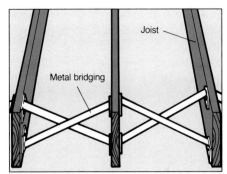

Metal bridging in standard sizes can be used to strengthen joists. Nail pairs in place every 8 feet or so.

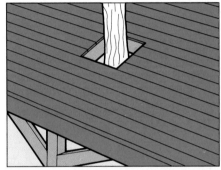

2. Cut decking to fit the box made by the added joists. Be sure to leave enough room for the tree to grow.

A STEPPED-DECK DESIGN

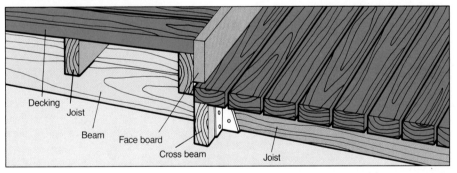

Decking Joist Beam Face board Cross beam Joist

To join two deck levels with a moderate-height step, hang the lower joists to a cross beam attached to the upper level beam ends. The lower decking lies at right angles to the upper.

STEPPED DECKS

You can build decks with stepped levels by attaching the joists of the lower level to the beams of the higher. The simplest method is to attach a cross beam to the upper level and hang the joists for the lower level to that facing beam. This construction can be used to make gradual steps down from a deck, rather than building the standard type of stairs.

STEP 8
PUTTING DOWN THE DECKING

When the joists are in place and braced, the decking can be installed. The most common type is 2 × 4s laid flat; 2 × 2s and 2 × 6s can also be used. An alternate method uses 2 × 4s set on edge. Always lay the bark side of the board up. To do this, look at the end of the piece: The curve of the grain should point down. Use 12-penny box or 16-penny casing nails set in a uniform pattern. To begin, lay a chalk line across all the joists, and align the decking with it. Drive nails in at opposing angles to prevent them from working out (nailing 2 × 4s on edge is shown at right). After putting down the first board, leave a space of ⅛ to ¼ inch between succeeding boards to allow moisture to pass through and to speed the drying of the surface. Put wedges or large nails between the boards to keep the spacing accurate.

Getting all the boards parallel is difficult. Keep checking alignment. If it is not exactly right, adjust the spacing gradually over the next two or three boards. When you are 6 feet or so from the end, put the last piece of decking down in line with the skirt and see how the remaining pieces fall into place. If in doubt, lay out all the boards before nailing them down.

SPLICING DECKING

If the deck boards do not reach the full deck width, cut them so that joints fall over a joist. Stagger the joints so they are not all on the same joist. The ends of every piece should be supported by a joist or by blocking.

SETTING THE NAILS

After laying the decking, you can use a nailset to drive all the nail heads below the surface of the boards. This is not absolutely necessary, but is a finishing detail. If you do it, fill each depression with wood putty.

STEP 9
TRIMMING THE DECKING

The last major step is trimming the decking. Before you trim, verify all of the dimensions and make sure that things are square. Small discrepancies can be absorbed in trimming. Use a chalk line to mark the cut line. Use a power saw to cut the board ends and keep it away from the skirt or joist to avoid marring the surface. Apply a coat of wood preservative to the cut ends of all the deck boards.

To cap the cut ends of the decking, as well as to provide an attractive edging strip, attach pieces of 1 × 3 or 2 × 3 across them. Try to use pieces long enough to avoid splicing, and nail them into each piece of decking so that no end can creep up over time.

LAYING THE DECKING

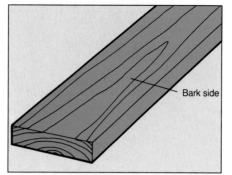

Install the decking so that the end grain curves downward, thus placing the bark side up.

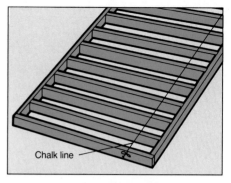

Use a chalk line to mark joist tops as a guide for keeping decking boards parallel.

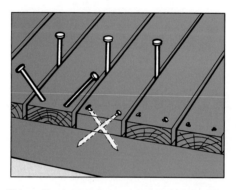

Drive nails at an angle to anchor decking boards to joists. Use large nails as temporary spacers.

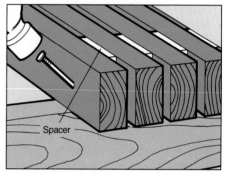

Toenail decking boards laid on edge to joists. Use thin wood pieces as spacers.

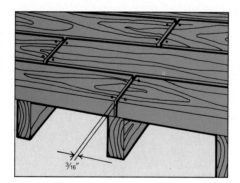

Splice decking pieces only on top of joists. Leave a ³⁄₁₆″ gap. Stagger splices.

Drive nail heads below the decking surface with a nail set. Fill the holes with wood filler.

TRIMMING THE DECKING

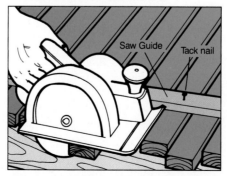

Cut off the protruding ends of decking pieces with a saw. Tacknail a guide board in place.

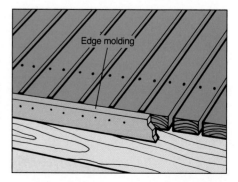

Nail long facing strips of thin lumber as edge molding to conceal the ends of the decking.

Wood Deck Maintenance

MAINTENANCE PROBLEMS

Even a well-built deck has problems. The accumulation of dirt, leaves, and moisture leads to wood decay. The problem is aggravated in damp climates. Shade and moisture encourage mildew and fungus. Normal wear and tear may loosen joints and connections and damage wood surfaces. Wood color and texture deteriorate through the weathering effects of sun, rain, freezing, and thawing, as well as through normal use. Long life for a wood deck begins with the good design and construction techniques described previously. In addition a deck needs proper care.

MAINTENANCE PROCEDURES

To give your deck longer life, follow these maintenance procedures:

1. Sweep the deck often; hose it down when dirt accumulates,

2. Clean the cracks between deck boards in the fall when the leaves have fallen, and in the spring before the busy season. Use a stiff wire or a putty knife.

3. Remove mildew promptly. It can appear as dirtlike spots, but grows into larger black or brown stains. Use a mildewcide annually or more often on shaded areas.

4. Check annually for wood rot and replace any damaged pieces. Coat any new pieces and cuts with wood preservative.

5. To restore the natural color of wood, brush on a dilute solution of oxalic acid. Add 4 ounces of acid to a gallon of water; use rubber gloves. When this solution has dried, hose off the deck thoroughly.

6. To accelerate the weathering process, or to match new wood to weathered wood, apply a solution of one part baking soda in five parts water. Wash the deck down the following day.

CLEANING THE DECK

Scrub down the deck surface at least twice a year, especially after the leaves fall, to remove dirt and decaying matter.

Dig dirt and rotting leaves out of the cracks between decking boards before the boards themselves begin to decay.

REPAIRING THE DECKING

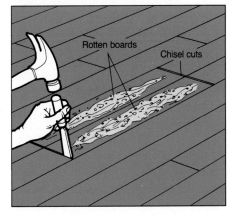

Chisel out all sections of rotting boards with a wood chisel and hammer. Cut new pieces to fit and coat them with wood preservative.

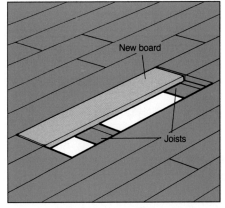

Nail new boards securely in place. The ends of all pieces should be nailed to joists or to blocking added between joists.

PRESERVING THE DECKING

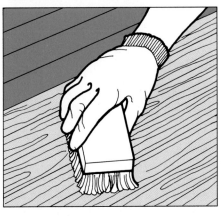

Brush on a dilute solution of oxalic acid to restore natural wood color. Wear gloves and goggles for protection.

In areas of severe weather, and for decks that get heavy use, apply a coat of wood preservative, stain or water repellent every two years or so.

6 VARIATIONS IN DECK CONSTRUCTION

A wood deck is an adaptable construction. The dimensions and shape of the standard design, as well as the building techniques described in Chapter 5, can be fitted to almost any plan. Several of the most common variations are described in this chapter.

A widely used construction technique for wood decks involves supporting one side of the deck against the house. Specifically, the piers and footings at one edge of the deck are replaced by a ledger beam that is firmly attached to the house framing. This technique is described on pages 95–98. Frequently, a low-level or ground-level deck can be attached to a ledger beam and supported directly on the footings.

One advantage of standard deck construction is that it does not need a level or regular ground surface for successful application. A raised deck can be built on otherwise useless terrain. This does, however, require additional bracing and otherwise strengthened construction, as spelled out on pages 99–102. This type of deck can also be attached to a house, using a ledger beam.

The simplest of decks, a modular parquet design, is described on page 103. This construction can even be used as a temporary deck, if your building plans are likely to change.

For other design variations, such as decks over water, load-bearing decks, and cantilevered decks, get the advice of a professional architect or contractor.

A DECK SUPPORTED ON A LEDGER

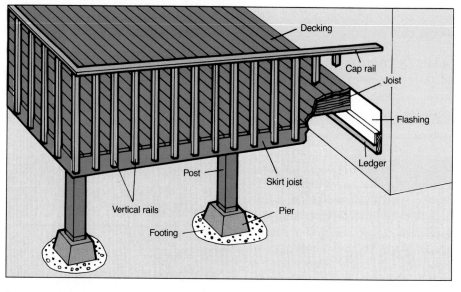

The joists of this deck rest on a ledger that is bolted to the house; this eliminates the row of posts and the beam that would otherwise be needed to support that side of the deck.

A RAISED DECK

Extended posts support one side of this raised deck; the other side is attached to the house.

A PARQUET DECK

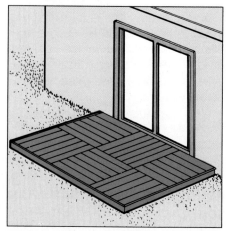

Modular units make up this simple deck, which is laid directly on the ground.

Building a Ledger-Supported Deck

Attaching a wood deck to your house or another structure can save time and money; when the house supports one end of the deck, you eliminate posts and beams along one side of the deck. In addition, this connection ensures that the house and deck will work together over the years. However, there are some disadvantages: 1. The connection to the house requires careful attention, particularly to the leveling of the deck in relation to the house. 2. The deck may settle faster than the house, causing strain or separation at the connection. 3. If the deck is in a northern climate, the wood may expand and contract, causing minor structural failure of the joists attached to the house wall.

STEP 1
PLANNING THE DECK

If you decide that attaching the deck to the house is desirable, read and apply the planning procedures discussed in chapters 1 through 4.

If your deck is to be built over an existing set of concrete steps, you may leave the top of the steps as an entry space just outside the door or cover the stairs completely with the decking. Both these options are illustrated at right. If the steps are wood, it is a good idea to remove them completely, so that the joists of the new deck are all attached directly to the house itself.

STEP 2
SITE PREPARATION

When your plan is complete and approved by local authorities, proceed with the site preparation, described in Step 1 on page 82.

STEP 3
ATTACHING THE LEDGER

A deck is attached to another structure, such as a house by attaching a ledger to the house and then connecting the deck joists to the ledger. A ledger is a piece of lumber the same size as the deck joists. Your local building code may specify the size, but for a deck

BUILDING A DECK OVER EXISTING STEPS

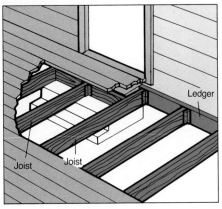

If the top step is below the desired deck level, the decking can be laid continuously across the step as in a standard deck.

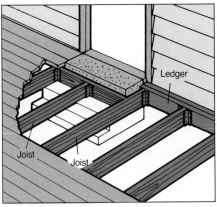

If the top step is at the desired level, the decking must be fitted around the step, with joist support provided on all sides.

LOCATING A HEADER

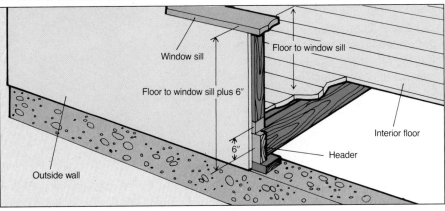

To find a header in wood house construction, transfer inside measurements to the outside wall at a window sill location, as explained in the text on page 96.

SETTING A LEDGER IN PLACE

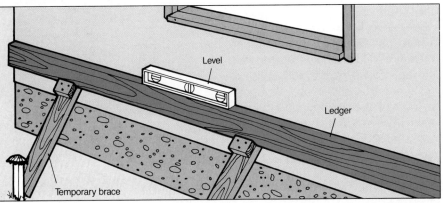

Place the ledger against the house at the level determined in the previous step, holding it in place with temporary braces. Use a carpenter's level to place the ledger accurately.

about 75 square feet or larger, use a 2 × 8 or a 2 × 10. The deck joists can sit on top of the ledger or they can be attached level with the top, using metal joist hangers. The choice depends on where the ledger can best be attached to the house. If you have a brick or masonry foundation, you can choose either method. If you are attaching the ledger to the header of a wood construction, it is best to use joist hangers.

ATTACHING THE LEDGER TO WOOD SUPPORT

The ledger should be securely fastened to the floor header, not to studs or to exterior siding. The header is exposed on some houses. If it isn't, find the inside floor level at a door or by measuring down to the floor from an inside window sill and transfer that measurement to the outside wall. Measure down 6 inches more: this point is the middle of the header.

Brace the ledger up against the header or the mark. The top of the decking should be at least 1 inch below a door opening to keep water out. So place the top of the ledger 1 inch plus the thickness of the decking below the door. Tack-nail the ledger to the header and make sure it is level. Then install lag screws or bolts no more than 24 inches apart. (You can use bolts if you can reach from the inside to add washers and nuts.) Drill through the ledger into the header, and use a wrench to tighten the screws or bolts.

ATTACHING THE LEDGER TO MASONRY

Use temporary 2 × 4 braces with cleats to hold the ledger up against a masonry or concrete wall. Check that the ledger is level and drill holes through it no more than 24 inches apart; then use a masonry bit to drill holes into the wall. Use lag screws, expansion bolts, or stud anchors as shown at right. Check the level of the ledger again as you tighten bolts or screws with a wrench. If necessary, loosen the connectors and adjust the ledger.

STEP 4
INSTALLING PROTECTIVE FLASHING

If moisture collects between the ledger

ATTACHING A LEDGER TO WOOD SUPPORT

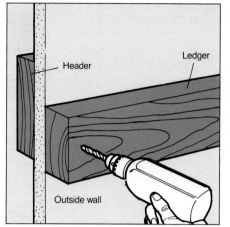

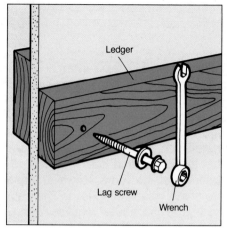

Drill holes through the ledger and outside wall into the header about 24 inches apart. Lag screws should not penetrate the far side of the header.

Use a wrench to drive the lag screws into the header, or to tighten lag bolts. Use washers with both screws and bolts.

ATTACHING A LEDGER TO A BRICK WALL

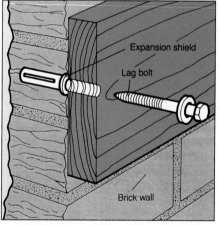

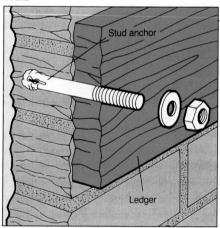

Drill holes through the ledger into the wall with a masonry bit. Remove the ledger and install expansion shields. Secure the ledger with lag bolts.

A ledger may be attached to a brick wall by drilling the holes and driving stud anchors in place. Secure the ledger with washers and nuts.

SHAPING FLASHING

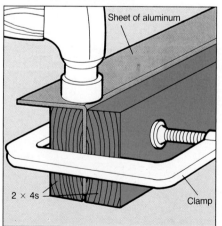

INSTALLING FLASHING

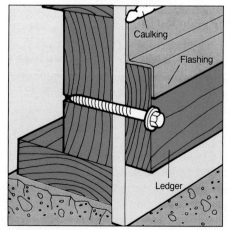

Form a strip of aluminum sheeting into the desired shape by clamping it between a pair of 2 × 4s and bending it with careful hammer blows.

Attach flashing to the top of the ledger with nails, and seal the top edge of the flashing with exterior-grade caulking.

and the house, decay can result. If you live in a rainy area, prevent this by installing flashing, a strip of aluminum or galvanized metal shaped to lead water away from the joint.

To find the width of flashing you need, add the thickness of the decking to the width of the ledger, plus 1 inch. If the joists sit on top of the ledger, add their width. Bend the flashing strips into the shapes shown at right, by clamping a strip between two 2 × 4s and carefully pounding out a right angle with a hammer and block of wood.

FLASHING AGAINST SIDING

If the siding is flush, nail the flashing through it, into the wall studs, and seal the top with a bead of exterior-grade or silicone caulking. If the house has shingles or lap siding, slip the flashing under the siding and nail it to the studs; seal the joint with caulking.

FLASHING ON STUCCO

If the wall is stucco, mark a cutting line across it just below the top of the decking. Use a circular saw with an abrasive blade to cut a slot about 3/8 inch deep in the stucco. Bend the top edge of the flashing to fit into this slot; seal the joint.

FLASHING AGAINST MASONRY

If the deck is against brick or concrete, nail the flashing to the top of the ledger or use masonry nails to nail it to the house. Caulk behind the flashing to fill all gaps, nail it, and caulk the top edge and nail heads.

FLASHING BEHIND JOISTS

If your deck joists sit on top of the ledger beams, be sure to cut the flashing wide enough to reach up above the joist tops. Attach the flashing and caulk it as described above.

AN ALTERNATE METHOD

A simpler way to prevent water damage to the ledger is to install five or six metal washers on each mounting lag screw or bolt, between the house and the header. This provides enough space for water to run down freely, without getting trapped, and for air to circulate to dry the wood surfaces.

FLASHING UNDER SHINGLES

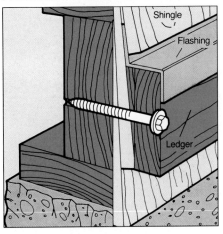

If your house is shingled, slip the top edge of the flashing under the shingles above the ledger beam. Nail the flashing to the ledger.

FLASHING OVER BRICK

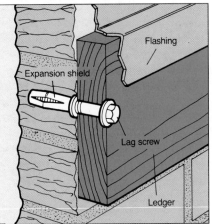

Fill mortar joints between bricks flush to the surface with caulking. Nail the flashing to the ledger top, or to the wall with masonry nails. Caulk the wall-flashing joint.

INSTALLING FLASHING OVER STUCCO

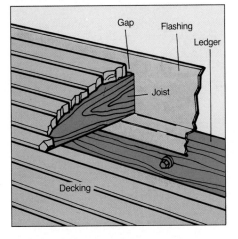

1. Cut a slot 3/8 inch deep in the stucco an inch or two above the ledger, using a circular saw with a carbide blade.

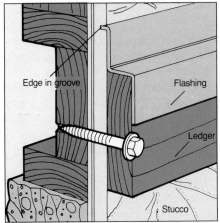

2. Bend the top edge of the flashing strip to fit the slot. Nail the flashing to the ledger and caulk the joint at the stucco.

FLASHING BEHIND JOISTS

If the joists rest on top of the ledger, be sure the flashing rises high enough to protect joist ends. Attach flashing as described above.

MOUNTING WITH WASHERS

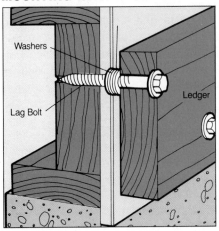

Place four or five washers between ledger and wall on each bolt; this creates an air gap that eliminates the need for flashing.

STEP 5
INSTALLING FOOTINGS, POSTS, AND BEAMS

The first steps in building the supporting framework of a ledger-supported deck are like those for the freestanding deck described in detail on pages 83–92. They are summarized here. Locate the positions of the posts by setting up batter boards and running lines to mark the dimensions of the deck. Use the 3-4-5 triangle method to make sure the corners are right angles. Make the footings as described on page 84 and set up the posts. Attach the beams (see pages 87–90). Be sure that the beam tops are progressively lower than the ledger, working outward from the house, so the deck will slope slightly away for good drainage.

SUPPORTING A LOW-LEVEL DECK

When the interior floor level is between 12 and 25 inches above ground level, the beams can rest directly on the footings; posts are not needed. The diagram at right shows how to do this.

STEP 6
PLACING JOISTS ON TOP OF THE LEDGER

If your joists rest on top of the ledger and beams, they may be attached by toenailing or by using a saddle anchor or hurricane anchor to make a secure connection (page 89).

HANGING JOISTS BETWEEN BEAM AND LEDGER

To install joist tops at the same level as the beam and ledger tops, use joist hangers to secure the joists in place (see page 90). If your joists are more than 8 feet long, add bracing, as described on page 101.

STEP 7
INSTALLING THE DECKING

Decking patterns are described on pages 36 and 42; nailing techniques are explained on pages 91–92. Decking should be installed parallel to the house, as shown at right. Allow a ½-inch gap between the house wall and the first piece of decking. Trim the outer edges of the decking as described on page 92.

LOCATING DECK POSTS ON THE GROUND

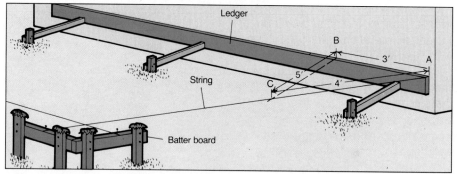

Batter boards support strings that mark the position of deck posts. A string can be run at right angles to the house by setting up a triangle with 3-, 4- and 5-foot sides, as shown above.

BUILDING A DECK WITHOUT POSTS

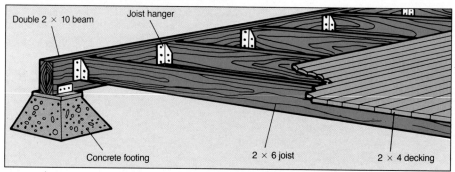

If posts are not needed, place the beams directly on the footings, securing them with metal connectors. The beams can be single pieces or doubled joist lumber, as shown above.

ATTACHING JOISTS TO A LEDGER

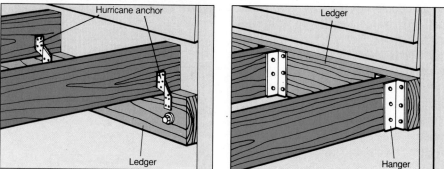

If joists rest on top of the ledger (left), attach them securely with hurricane anchors. If joists hang down level with the ledger top, use joist hangers to join joist to ledger.

INSTALLING THE DECKING

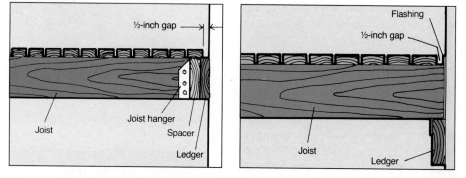

Whether the joists hang down level with the joist top (left) or are mounted on top of the ledger, leave a 1-inch gap between the wall and the decking.

Building a Raised Deck

A wood deck can be built up to about 12 feet above grade using the designs and construction techniques explained in chapters 1 through 5. The highest strength 4 × 4 wood posts (see chart on page 30) will be adequate if the load-bearing area—the area supported by four posts or two posts and a ledger—is no more than 80 square feet. To support larger areas, or when using weaker wood, use larger posts. If you plan a deck higher than 12 feet or a deck that will support heavy loads, consult an architect or contractor. Check local building codes for limitations and support requirements.

A raised deck can be freestanding, but if you attach one side to a house or other structure, the deck will have greater stability. Two designs are shown here, a relatively simple, small deck built on stable, flat ground, and a larger deck built on sloping ground. You'll need a helper for either project.

ATTACHING DECK TO SECOND STORY
STEP 1
INSTALLING THE LEDGER

Attach a ledger beam (2 × 8 or 2 × 10) to the second-story header, as described on pages 95 and 96. Level it and use ¼ × 3½-inch lag screws no more than 24 inches apart.

STEP 2
MAKING THE JOIST SKIRT

Cut two skirt joists to the required length and nail them to the ledger ends, using three 10- or 16-penny nails. Make a temporary support of 2 × 4s for the outside end of these joists. Slope the joists down from the ledger, ⅛ inch per foot. Cut and install the third skirt joist. Use a diagonal 2 × 4 to hold the completed skirt square.

STEP 3
HANGING THE INSIDE JOISTS

Install the remaining joists on 18- or 24-inch centers (see decking chart on page 30). You can hang the joists from a cleat nailed to the ledger and the outer skirt, or from metal hangers.

A DESIGN FOR A SECOND-STORY DECK

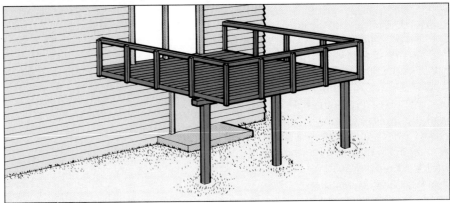

This deck stands about 10 feet above grade, supported at one end by a ledger attached to the house, and at the other end by a beam attached to a row of posts 4 to 6 feet apart. Sliding glass doors have replaced the original small window shown in the construction illustrations below.

ATTACHING THE LEDGER

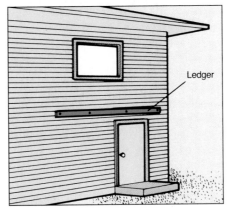

Drill holes into a wood or masonry wall so that lag screws can be used to attach the ledger. Make sure the ledger is level.

MAKING THE SKIRT

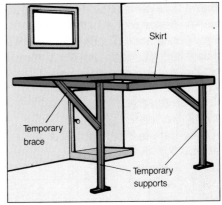

Two side skirt joists are attached to the ledger; temporary supports hold them up while the outside skirt joist is installed.

METHODS FOR ATTACHING THE JOISTS

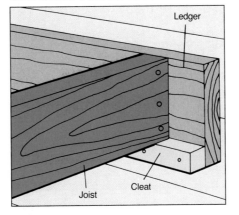

Joists can rest on wood cleats that are nailed or screwed to the bottom edge of the ledger; toenail the joists to the ledger.

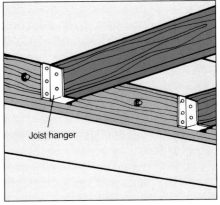

Joists can also be attached to the ledger by means of metal hangers that are nailed to both ledger and joist.

STEP 4
ATTACHING THE BEAM

Cut a 4 × 6 (or two joists nailed together) to fit the width of the deck; snap a chalk line across the underside of the joists at the desired beam location. The joists can overhang the beam one-quarter of their length (see page 43). Attach the beam to each joist, including the skirt joists, with a metal connector.

STEP 5
LOCATING THE FOOTINGS

Mark the post positions on the underside of the beam and drop a plumb line from each position to the ground to find the location of the footing holes. Mark these spots with stakes.

STEP 6
DIGGING THE FOOTING HOLES

Dig holes at each of the stakes (you can rent a posthole digger for this chore). The holes should be at least 24 inches deep; in areas of freezing and thawing the bottom should be 8 inches below the frost line. The holes should be 12 to 14 inches in diameter (check local codes).

STEP 7
HANGING AND BRACING THE POSTS

Cut the posts to reach down to the frost line; there should be 8 to 10 inches between the bottom of the post and the bottom of the hole. Coat all post ends with preservative. Attach the posts to the beams with metal connectors. Brace the posts with scraps of wood staked in the ground. Make sure the posts are vertical. (Exterior posts can be extended to support a railing; see Chapter 7.)

STEP 8
POURING THE FOOTINGS

Mix up enough concrete to make the footings (see pages 86–87). Pour the concrete around the posts; be careful not to move the posts out of line. Mound the concrete up around the posts two or three inches above grade to provide drainage. Let the concrete cure for three days before removing the bracing.

HANGING THE BEAM

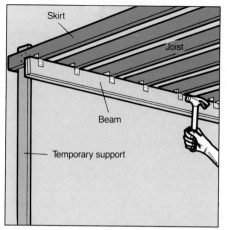

The single beam is attached to the underside of each joist, including the skirt joists, with metal connectors nailed to both members.

DIGGING FOOTING HOLES

Use a posthole digger to dig holes at the staked positions. Follow local codes for the depth and diameter of the holes.

POURING THE FOOTINGS

Fill the holes around the posts with concrete; make sure the posts remain vertical. Keep the braces in position until the concrete cures.

LOCATING FOOTINGS

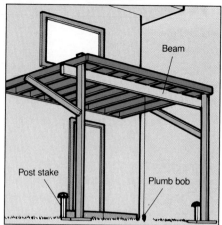

Drop a plumb line from the points on the beam where you intend to attach the posts. Where the line touches the ground, drive a stake.

INSTALLING POSTS

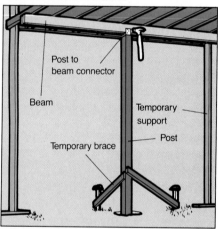

Hang the posts in the holes and attach them to the beam with metal connectors. Hold them securely in position with temporary braces.

LAYING THE DECKING

Nail decking to the joists, parallel to the house, with two nails into each joist. Start at the house, with a 1-inch gap to the first board.

STEP 9
INSTALLING THE DECKING

Nail down the decking parallel to the house, beginning at the house. Leave a 1-inch gap between decking and wall. Use a large nail or a scrap of wood to space the decking boards about ¼ inch apart. Countersink the nailheads and fill the holes with putty (see page 92).

STEP 10
TRIMMING THE DECKING

When all the decking has been installed, snap a chalk line across the ends of the pieces at the desired place, or tack down a straight board as a saw guide. Trim the ends off along the line with a circular saw. Apply a coat of preservative to the newly cut ends.

BRACING A RAISED DECK

If your deck stands more than 4 feet off the ground, the posts should be braced to provide stability.

If the deck is supported by only two posts and attached to a ledger beam, the posts should be braced to the joists. To brace the deck shown here, cut two pieces of 2 × 4 or 2 × 6 and attach them from the post to the inside of the skirt joist. The braces should be placed at a 45-degree angle, and the tops should be no more than 2 feet from the post. Cut the ends of the braces so that they stand vertical; this prevents moisture accumulation and the resulting wood decay. Cut the ends of the braces flush with post and joist. Use bolts or lag screws to install the braces. It may be necessary to insert blocking between the brace and the post and/or the joist.

If more than two posts support the deck, the braces should run from post to post. Bracing should be installed in a continuous pattern all around the deck so that all outside posts are connected. The K-pattern bracing shown at right is a strong design. You can install two braces extending across three posts in an X pattern if desired. Cut all brace ends vertically. Where two braces meet, leave a ½-inch space between them for air circulation. Install braces with lag screws or bolts.

Information on railings is presented in Chapter 7, and information on stairs is presented in Chapter 8.

SPACING THE DECKING

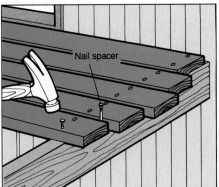

Temporarily insert large nails or wood scrap between decking pieces so that there is a constant ¼-inch spacing across the deck.

TRIMMING THE DECKING

Use a circular saw to trim the ends of the decking. Be careful to keep the saw blade away from the skirt joists.

BRACING FOR DECK POSTS

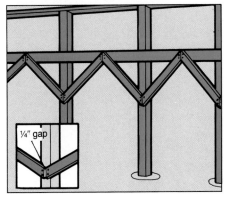

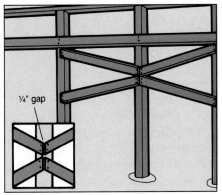

Deck posts can be braced by screwing or bolting braces between posts and joists (left) or between posts (right). Insets show how ends of all braces should be cut vertical and a ¼-inch gap left to prevent moisture accumulation.

AN ALTERNATE RAISED DECK DESIGN

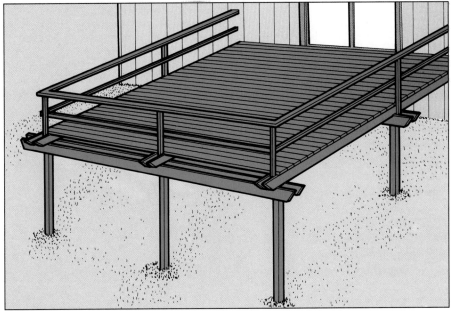

This deck is designed for sloping or uneven ground. The posts are installed first; beams and joists of doubled lumber are then attached to the sides of the posts. The posts can be extended up to support the railing, if desired.

AN ALTERNATE DESIGN

The variations described here are useful for a raised deck that requires two or more rows of posts, or one built on sloping or unstable ground. One side is attached to the house for stability.

STEP 1
INSTALLING THE LEDGER

Attach the ledger securely (see pages 95–96). Be sure it is level.

STEP 2
SETTING UP THE POSTS

Find the post hole locations as described on pages 83–84. Dig down to stable ground, below the frost line if local codes require it. Put at least 6 inches of gravel in each hole. Cut 4 × 4 posts a few inches higher than the joist tops. Set the posts in the holes and brace them with scraps of wood. Fill with concrete and let cure for two days.

STEP 3
ATTACHING THE SUPPORT BLOCKS

Run lines from the ledger and mark the joist-top locations on the posts. Measure down from the marks a distance equal to the depth of the joists plus the depth of the beams, and mark a line for the tops of the support blocks. Attach blocks to both sides of all posts.

STEP 4
INSTALLING BEAMS AND JOISTS

Cut a pair of beams for each row of posts and enough joists for proper decking support (see charts, pages 30 and 34). Rest the beams on the blocks and attach them to the posts with lag screws. Rest the joists on the beams. Attach them to the ledger with hangers, and to the posts with lag screws. Cut all inside post tops flush with joists.

STEP 5
INSTALLING THE DECKING

Nail down the decking and trim the edges as described on pages 91–92.

STEP 6
BRACING THE POSTS

Attach 2 × 4 or 2 × 6 bracing to all outside posts; see page 101.

ATTACHING A LEDGER

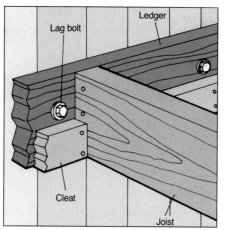

The ledger is bolted to the house studs or a masonry wall. The joist is notched at the bottom and rests on a cleat nailed to the ledger.

FILLING POST HOLES

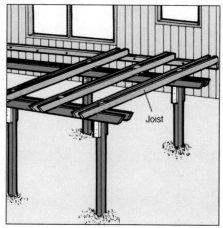

Posts should rest on about 6 inches of gravel in holes at least 3 feet deep. When the posts are securely braced, the holes are filled with gravel or concrete.

INSTALLING THE JOISTS

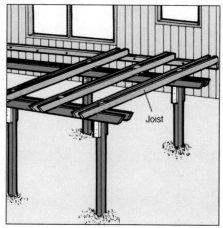

Rest joists on the ledger (see Step 1) and on the beams at both sides of the posts. Screw or bolt the joists to the beams.

BRACING THE POSTS

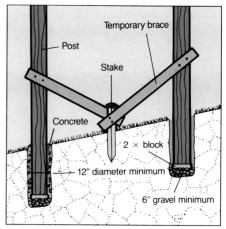

Dig post holes only in stable ground; they must extend below frost level. Set posts in the holes, braced so they stay vertical.

ATTACHING BLOCKS AND BEAMS

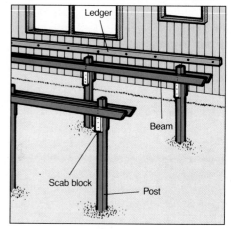

Screw or bolt scab blocks to each side of the posts so there is room above them for both beams and joists. Make sure beams are level.

LAYING THE DECKING

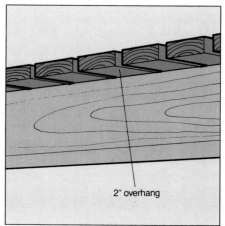

Lay decking boards on the joists parallel to the house. Use two nails per joist, with ¼-inch spacing between boards. Trim to a 2-inch overhang.

Building a Modular Parquet Deck

These instructions explain how to build a very simple deck directly on level, well-drained ground. This project builds a 12 × 12-foot deck, using 3-foot parquet squares. It can be modified to fit other shapes and dimensions, still using modular squares.

MATERIALS LIST

Qty	Size	Length	Use
32	2 × 4	3 ft	cleats
144	2 × 4	3 ft	decking

38 cubic feet of gravel; 38 cubic feet of sand; about 8¼ lbs 10d nails; saw, hammer, shovel, soil tamper, rake.

STEP 1
CUTTING THE LUMBER
Cut 176 pieces of 2 × 4 lumber, each 3 feet long. Sand off all rough edges. Use treated wood or heart cedar.

STEP 2
MAKING THE SQUARES
Make a nailing jig out of scrap lumber, with inside dimensions of 36 × 36 inches. Place 3-foot lengths of 2 × 4s at opposite sides of the jig and nail nine 2 × 4 decking pieces to the cleats with two 10-penny nails at each end. Nail the first and last pieces in place to begin. Then space the remaining seven members equally. Repeat until you have 16 parquet squares.

STEP 3
PREPARING THE SITE
Use the 3-4-5 triangulation method (pages 83–84) to mark out the deck site. Remove soil within the site lines to a depth of 6 inches. Lay 3 inches of gravel on the bottom and level it with a rake. Spread 3 inches of sand over the gravel and tamp it down level.

STEP 4
PLACING THE SQUARES
Lay the parquet squares in place, alternating the direction of the decking. Toenail them together. Fill the outside edge of the excavation with sand to ground level and tamp it down.

MAKING THE MODULES IN A JIG

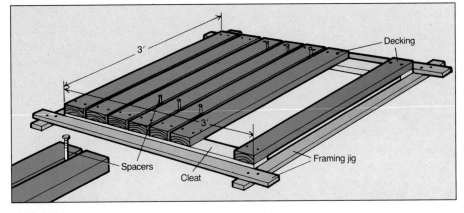

Set the cleats against opposite sides of the framing jig and nail nine decking pieces to the cleats so that they are evenly spaced across the module.

LAYING OUT THE DECK SITE

Outline the deck area to be excavated with strings stretched between stakes. Measure triangles with 3-, 4- and 5-foot sides at the corners to make sure that each corner is a right angle.

INSTALLING THE DECK MODULES

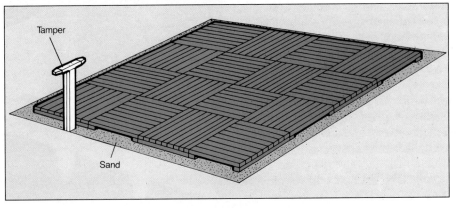

Set the modules in position on the sand-filled excavation. Backfill the space around the modules with sand and tamp it firmly in place. You can make a tamper out of 2 × 4s.

7 RAILINGS AND BENCHES

Railings on a wood deck perform several functions: They add a finishing touch to the deck; they provide safety; and, in combination with benches, they form built-in furniture that makes the deck attractive and more useful.

Local building codes usually specify which decks require railings and how high the railings must be. In general, any deck that stands more than 24 inches above grade must have a railing, although sometimes a deck height up to 30 inches is allowed. Railings usually must be 36 inches high; for some high-level decks a 42-inch height is specified. Check your code first.

In any case, a railing must be made of durable wood and must be strong enough to support people leaning or sitting on it. A combination of 4 × 4 posts and 2 × 4 rails can provide an excellent railing. This design is economical and it lets you fill in the space between posts and rails in any way you desire.

The varieties of railings are endless. Two methods of supporting railings are shown here: connecting them to extended deck posts, and attaching them to joists. A railing should have no openings larger than 9 or 10 inches square, to prevent small children from falling through. Avoid any joints where rain can collect and cause wood decay. Assemble railings with lag screws, bolts, and metal connectors instead of nails. If you put a solid fill-in between posts, leave a 3-inch opening at the bottom for easy cleaning.

A RAILING ATTACHED TO RAISED DECK POSTS

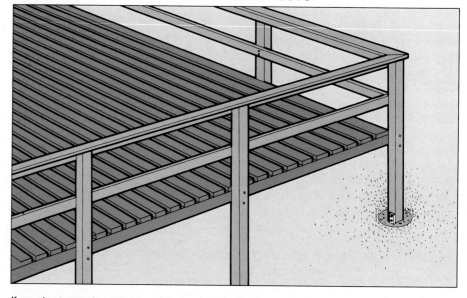

If you plan to attach a railing to extended deck posts, the deck beams will have to be attached to the inner sides of the posts; this procedure is explained on page 88.

A RAILING ATTACHED TO THE JOISTS

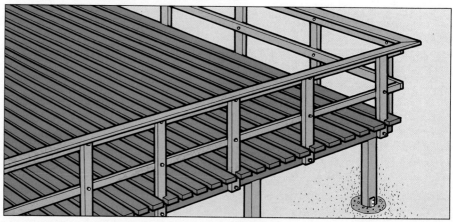

Railing posts may be bolted to the sides of the joists, including skirt joists (opposite page). They may also be attached to the ends of joists, as shown on page 106.

ATTACHING RAILING TO EXTERIOR DECK POSTS

STEP 1
CUTTING THE POSTS

If you want the posts that support the perimeter of the deck to support a railing also, use 4 × 4s long enough to extend the distance above the decking required by code. After the decking is installed cut off these posts at the railing height minus the cap board thickness (see Step 2).

STEP 2
INSTALLING CAP BOARDS

The simplest cap is made of 2 × 4s screwed or nailed to the tops of the 4 × 4 posts. Center any splices directly over a post, using a butt joint. Miter two boards that join over a corner post. You can also use 2 × 6s as caps, with a reinforcing 2 × 4 beneath.

STEP 3
ATTACHING HORIZONTAL RAILS

To strengthen the railing and fill in the open space, you can install 2 × 4s horizontally between the posts. Cut lengths to fit snugly and attach them with metal connectors, angle irons, or simple wood cleats. If more members are needed to make the railing sturdy or childproof, you can install additional 2 × 4s or 2 × 2s, either horizontally or vertically. Screw or bolt the fill-in pieces to the posts, or to the 2 × 4 cap boards and railings.

ATTACHING RAILING TO EXTERIOR JOISTS

STEP 1
ATTACHING 4 × 4 POSTS TO EXTERIOR JOISTS

Cut pieces of 4 × 4 to rise from the bottom of the joist to the height required by code, minus the thickness of the cap. Drill at least two bolt or screw holes at the bottom of the posts. Space the posts about 4 or 5 feet apart, and no more than 6 to 12 inches from the corners. Hold the posts vertically in position against the joist; hammer a bolt through the holes to mark the joist. Drill holes in the joist and attach the post.

JOINING CAP BOARD SECTIONS

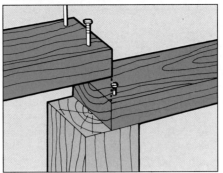

When attaching flat cap boards to post tops, make splices with a butt joint over the post.

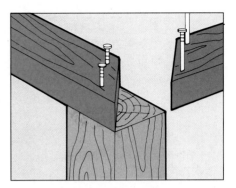

Attach ends of cap boards to a corner post top with a mitered butt joint. Drill pilot holes for all nailing near ends.

INSTALLING HORIZONTAL RAILS

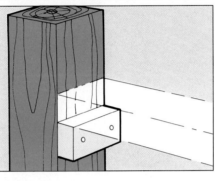

Horizontal rails may be supported on a wood cleat and toenailed to post and cleat.

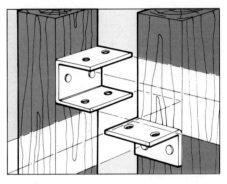

Attach rails to posts with metal connectors or angle irons for strong construction.

ATTACHING RAILING POSTS TO JOISTS

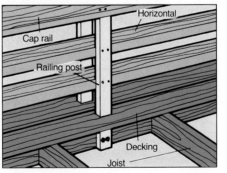

Double posts can be bolted to the joist and horizontal and cap rails nailed to both posts.

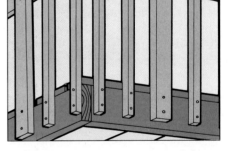

Alternating 2 × 4s and 2 × 2s can be bolted to the outsides of the skirt joists.

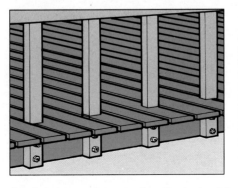

Sturdy 2 × 4 posts may need no other horizontal fill-in. Cut decking to fit around posts.

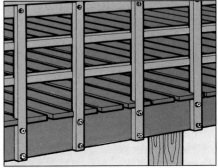

Lighter 2 × 2 posts need additional horizontal fill-in. Post-joist connection needs two bolts.

ALTERNATE METHOD
STEP 1
ATTACHING 2 × 4S OR 2 × 2S TO EXTERIOR JOISTS

To use 2 × 4s or 2 × 2s as railing posts, attach them to the exterior with bolts or lag screws. Space 2 × 2s about 10 inches apart, 2 × 4s 2 to 3 feet apart.

STEP 2
ATTACHING CAP BOARD AND RAILINGS

Attach 2 × 4s or 2 × 2s horizontally to the posts with bolts or lag screws. Make butt joints over the posts and mitered joints at the corners. Then attach cap boards to both the posts and the horizontal boards.

STEP 3
INSTALLING FILL-IN

If fill-in is needed to close up the open space, attach 2 × 2s horizontally to the posts with screws or bolts.

ALTERNATE RAILING DESIGNS

ATTACHING POSTS INSIDE DECK PERIMETER

Railing posts can be attached to a joist or a beam at almost any point inside the perimeter of the deck. Do this before the decking has been laid, and insert blocking between the joists to provide support for the ends of any decking pieces that abut the post. You can install a post anywhere on the deck if you provide enough support.

ATTACHING A RAILING TO EXTENDED JOISTS

In this design, the ends of the joists extend beyond the decking. (You may install all the joists this way or just those that support the railing posts.) Attach 2 × 4s in pairs, one on each side of the joist; use at least two bolts running through the three pieces. The cap board can be attached with metal connectors.

INSTALLING A SLANT RAILING

In this design variation, the posts are installed at an angle, either by cutting a notch in the post bottom and bolting it to the side of the joist or beam, or by bolting a pair of 2 × 4s at an angle to the end of an extended joist.

ATTACHING RAILING POSTS (CONTINUED)

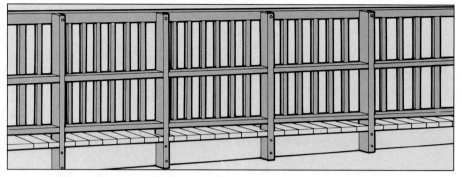

2 × 4s placed on edge may be bolted to joist sides. 1 × 1 vertical fill-in pieces are nailed to top, middle, and bottom horizontal rails.

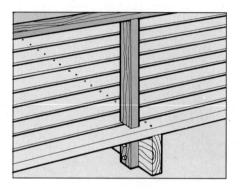

If railing posts are bolted to joist sides, decking must be cut to fit around posts.

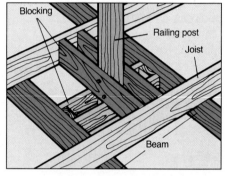

If a post cannot be bolted to an existing joist, additional support must be built in.

Shaped 1 × 4 railing posts can be bolted in pairs to the ends of joists. The cap rail is attached to each post with angle irons.

SLANTED RAILINGS ATTACHED TO JOISTS

Slanting posts with notched ends can be bolted on edge to outside joists.

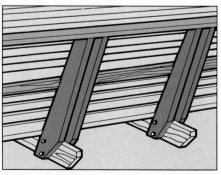

Slanting posts can also be bolted in pairs to the ends of joists.

ADDITIONAL FILL-IN DESIGNS

For a more solidly filled-in railing, attach 1× or 2× pieces horizontally in an alternating pattern, or apply sheets of plywood paneling. Leave 2 or 3 inches open at the bottom for drainage.

BUILDING A RAILING BENCH

STEP 1
INSTALLING THE SUPPORT

A simple bench can be added to a railing by installing two-piece seat supports and bolting them to the railing posts and the joists. Cut the decking to fit around the vertical member.

STEP 2
ATTACHING THE SEAT

Screw 2 × 6 boards to the seat supports. Make any splices in the seat with butt joints over the support, and add cleats underneath for more support.

INSTALLING A HEAVY BENCH

STEP 1
BUILDING THE SUPPORT

In a more solid bench design the back rest, a 2 × 12 set in at a comfortable angle, is supported by 2 × 6s bolted to each joist. The seat support is attached at the decking with metal angles.

STEP 2
MAKING THE SEAT

Screw 2 × 2s to the horizontal 2 × 4s that provide the seat support. Leave a ¼- or ½-inch space between the 2 × 2s. To splice the seating, make butt joints over the support and add cleats underneath for reinforcement.

BUILDING A LOW BENCH

STEP 1
INSTALLING THE SUPPORTS

To build a comfortable bench where there is no railing, bolt T-shaped supports made from 2 × 6s to the joists. Notch the decking to fit around them.

STEP 2
INSTALLING THE SEATS

Screw 2 × 2s, 2 × 3s, or 2 × 4s to the horizontal arm of the T-supports, leaving a ¼- or ½-inch space between the boards for drainage. For a decorative finish, screw 1 × 2s to the seat boards all around the perimeter of the bench.

RAILING FILL-IN DESIGNS

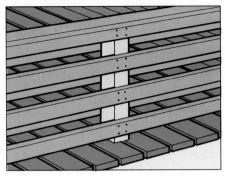

Long strips of 1 × 2 can be nailed to both sides of a 4 × 4 post.

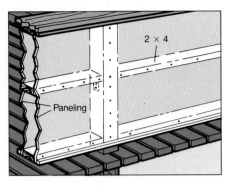

Panels of exterior-grade plywood nailed to horizontal 2 × 4s make a solid railing.

BUILDING A RAILING BENCH

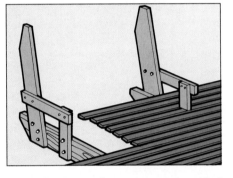

1. Make the support frames separately and bolt them to the ends of the joists.

2. Add seat and back boards. Finish the bench with a horizontal cap board.

BUILDING A HEAVY BENCH

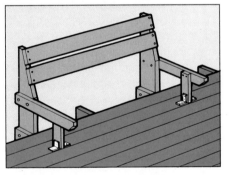

1. Bolt vertical supports to each joist. Attach seat supports to decking with angle irons.

2. Make the back from one 2 × 12 or two 2 × 6s. The seat is spaced 2 × 2s or 2 × 4s.

BUILDING A LOW BENCH

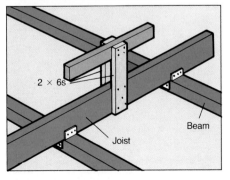

1. The T-support, made of three 2 × 6 pieces, is bolted to the joist.

2. The seat is made of pieces of 2x lumber screwed to the horizontal 2 × 6.

8 WOOD STAIRS AND RAMPS

Stairs provide access to a deck from the ground level or provide a connection between deck levels. If a deck is attached to a house, for convenience and safety, it is best to make the deck only an inch or two lower than the interior level.

The parts of a set of stairs are identified at right. The steps, called treads, are supported by the stringers, which are fastened at the top to the joists or beams of the deck and at ground level to a concrete footing.

Establishing the right relation between the height of the step, called the rise, and the depth of the tread, called the run, is important for safety. Stairs that are too tall or too shallow cause accidents. Follow this rule of thumb: The depth of the tread plus twice the step height or rise should equal about 25 inches. A good combination for outdoor steps is a 6-inch rise with a 12- or 13-inch tread. Another is a 6½-inch rise with an 11- or 12-inch tread. The deeper the tread, the lower the rise. In any case, all steps must have identical measurements. Steps of varied sizes cause stumbles.

A safe stairs must have a whole number of equal-size steps. Here is how to figure step dimensions and overall stair dimensions. Measure the total rise from ground level to deck level, the top surface of the decking; say it is 50 inches. Divide that by a convenient rise dimension, say 6

inches: $50 \div 6 = 8+$ steps, which rounds off to 8. To get the exact rise of each step, divide the total rise again, this time by the rounded-off step number: $50 \div 8 = 6¼$ inches. To determine how far from the deck edge the stairs will extend on the ground, figure the total run: Subtract 1 from the number of steps (the deck will be the tread of the top step), and multiply by an appropriate tread depth, say 12 inches. So the total run is: $(8 - 1) \times 12 = 84$ inches.

If you had rounded off the $8+$ step figure to 9 steps, the individual rise would be $50 \div 9 = 5½$ inches, and with a 14-inch tread the total run would be $(9 - 1) \times 14 = 112$ inches.

A 7-inch rise is about the safe max-

imum for outdoor steps, a 5-inch rise the safe minimum. Treads should be at least 11 inches deep. The width of the stairs depends on use. If most traffic will be one person at a time, 40 inches is adequate. If most traffic will be pairs or groups of people, provide at least a 5-foot width. The supporting stringers, cut from 2×10s or, preferably, 2×12s, should be placed no more than 30 inches apart. So, for example, stairs 5 feet wide need three stringers. For a total run of more than 6 feet, use the stronger double-stringer design shown on page 111. Treat all lumber surfaces, fresh cuts, and bolt holes with preservative. Check building codes for local requirements in dimensions and railings (see page 112) as well as design.

STAIR COMPONENTS

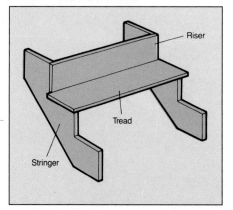

Standard wood stairs consist of the three basic components identified here.

STAIR DIMENSIONS

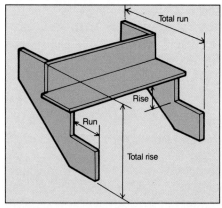

These are standard stair dimension names used in this chapter.

MAKING SIMPLE BOX STEPS

To join two deck levels separated by a rise of less than 20 inches, or to provide access to a low-level deck, use simple boxlike steps. If the total rise is no more than 14 inches, make one box step equal to half the rise. For a rise of no more than 19½ inches, make a two-step box. Toenail the steps to the deck levels, or provide a concrete slab for support.

BUILDING CLOSED-RISER STAIRS

For stairs with a total rise of between 19½ inches and 6 feet, use the notched stringer design shown here.

STEP 1
CUTTING STRINGERS

Establish the rise and tread dimensions as explained on page 108. Use a carpenter's square to mark the rise and run of each step on a 2 × 12. Start by marking a run at the top. When you cut out the marked pattern, cut the top end of the 2 × 12 parallel to the rise; cut the bottom parallel to the tread. Cut as many identical stringers as required by the stair width.

STEP 2
MAKING THE FOOTING

To build a support for the bottom end of the stringers, excavate a 6- to 8-inch-deep trench that extends about 6 inches beyond the sides of the steps and 8 to 10 inches in front. Line the rim with a frame of 2× lumber. Tilt the frame slightly away from the deck to provide drainage for the footing. Fill the trench with concrete, level it, and put anchoring hardware in place.

An alternate footing consists of a piece of 4 × 4 for each stringer, set into the concrete so the stringer side can be bolted to it.

STEP 3
ATTACHING THE STRINGERS

If the stringers run at right angles to the joists, attach them with metal connectors. If the joists and stringers are parallel, bolt them together. Use only galvanized fasteners. Bolt the bottoms of the stringers to the metal connectors in the concrete, or to the 4 × 4 posts.

SIMPLE BOX STEPS

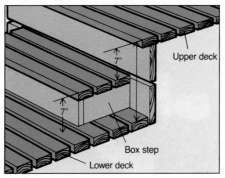

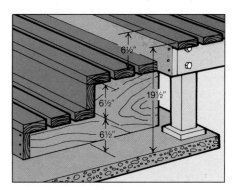

To fill a 14″ rise, make one 7″ box step: a three-sided frame of 2 × 6s with 2 × 4 treads.

To fill a 19½″ rise, make a two-step box. Cut two stringers from 2x lumber, as shown above.

STAIR STRINGERS

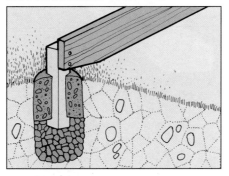

Mark two stringers for a closed-riser stairs as shown here, and cut out the notches.

STAIR FOOTING

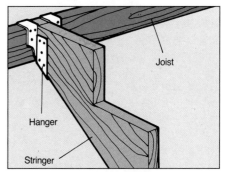

To make a footing for stringers, pour concrete into a form made of 2 × 6s; install hardware.

AN ALTERNATE FOOTING

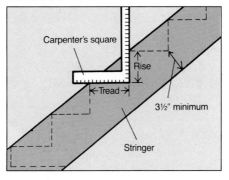

Dig two holes; place short 4 × 4 posts on gravel base and fill hole with concrete; bolt stringer to post.

ATTACHING TO SIDE

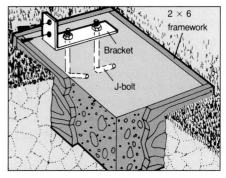

Use a metal hanger to attach the top of a stringer to the side of a joist.

ATTACHING TO END

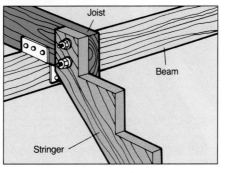

Use carriage bolts to secure the top of a stringer to the end of a joist.

ATTACHING TO FOOTING

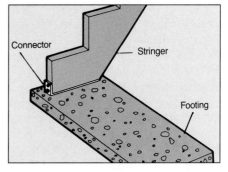

Secure the bottom end of the stringer to the hardware in the footing with screws or lag bolts.

STEP 4
CUTTING AND INSTALLING RISERS

Cut the risers from 2× lumber to fit the rise notches in the stringers exactly. The bottom of the riser rests on the stringer. Nail the risers in place with 12-penny galvanized nails. Note: The riser boards may be omitted if desired, to make a more open design.

STEP 5
CUTTING AND INSTALLING TREADS

Cut the treads from 2× lumber; a 1-inch overhang in front is standard. Use several 2 × 4s or 2 × 6s, rather than larger boards, which are more likely to warp. Leave a ½-inch space between boards. Nail the treads in place with galvanized 16-penny nails. Place the bark side of the treads up (page 92).

BUILDING CLEAT-SUPPORTED STAIRS

This alternate basic stair design involves attaching wood cleats to the stringers to support the treads, rather than cutting notches for them.

STEP 1
MARKING THE STRINGERS

Choose the riser and tread dimensions as explained on page 108. Use a carpenter's square to mark the rise and run of each step on a 2 × 12 (see Step 1 on page 109). Cut only the top and bottom ends of the stringers.

STEP 2
CUTTING AND ATTACHING CLEATS

Using 2 × 4 lumber, cut cleats to support the full depth of each tread on each stringer. Bolt the cleats to the inside of the stringers, aligned with the mark made in Step 1, but with a ⅛-inch forward tilt for drainage.

STEP 3
MAKING THE FOOTING

Make a footing to support the stair bottom, as described on page 109.

STEP 4
ATTACHING THE STRINGERS

Attach the stringers to the deck joists and to the footing (see page 109).

INSTALLING RISERS

Cut the risers to fit the stringers; the top of the riser must be flush with the horizontal stringer cut.

INSTALLING TREADS

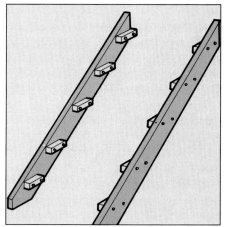

Make the treads from pieces of 2x lumber. You may leave a ½-inch overhang at the sides and at the front. Leave ½-inch space between pieces.

MAKING CLEAT-SUPPORTED STAIRS

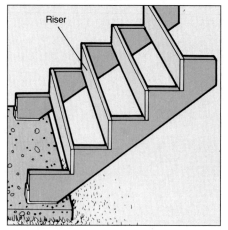

1. Mark the stringer as you did for a closed-riser stairs (page 109), but do not make any cuts except at both ends of the stringers.

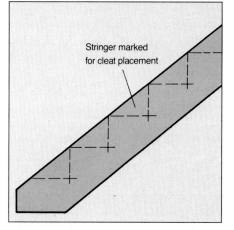

2. Bolt the cleats to the insides of both stringers so that the top of the cleat lies on the mark made in Step 1.

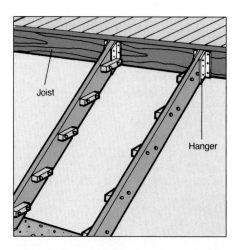

3. Attach the stringers to the joists and to the footing, using the methods described on page 109.

4. Cut 2 × 4s or 2 × 6s to fit between the stringers and screw them to the tops of the cleats. Leave ½-inch space between tread boards.

STEP 5
INSTALLING THE TREADS

Cut treads from 2 × 4 or 2 × 6 lumber to fit snugly between the stringers. Screw the treads to the top of the cleats. Leave ½ inch between tread boards.

BUILDING DOUBLE-STRINGER STAIRS

If the total run of your stairs is more than 6 feet, use double-stringer construction for additional support.

STEP 1
CUTTING AND JOINING THE STRINGERS

For each double stringer, cut one solid outer stringer, like that used for the cleat-supported steps (Step 1, page 110), and one notched inner stringer (Step 1, page 109). Nail the stringers together with 10-penny nails.

STEP 2
PROVIDING A FOOTING

Build a concrete footing to support the stair bottom (Step 2, page 109).

STEP 3
ATTACHING STRINGERS

Attach the top of the stringers to the joists (Step 3, page 109) and the bottoms to the footing.

STEP 4
CUTTING AND INSTALLING RISERS AND TREADS

Cut risers and treads from 2 × lumber to fit the notched stringer, and install as explained in Steps 4 and 5, page 110.

BUILDING A RAMP

A ramp may be an attractive design alternative to stairs or a necessity for a person in a wheelchair. Local codes may be very specific in the latter case. Usually the run of a ramp must be eight times the rise. For example, if the total rise is 3 feet, the total run must be at least 24 feet.

STEP 1
DESIGNING THE RAMP

A ramp may be placed at right angles to a deck if you have the space; if not, it can be built parallel to the deck, as shown at right, with a wide top landing. The ramp should be 4 feet wide, and usually requires railings (see page 112).

MAKING DOUBLE-STRINGER STAIRS

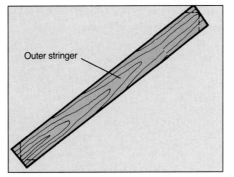

1. Mark two outer stringers to fit between joists and footing and cut the ends.

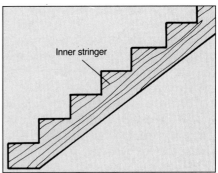

2. Cut two inner stringers to match the outer pair, then notch them for risers and treads.

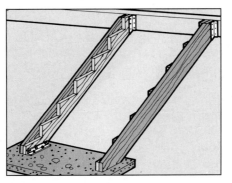

3. Nail or screw the stringer pairs together and attach them to the joist and the footing.

4. Cut treads to fit the inner stringer and nail them in place. Install risers if desired.

A DESIGN FOR A WOOD RAMP

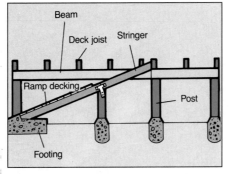

This elevation drawing of a ramp shows the stringers supported by footing, posts and joist.

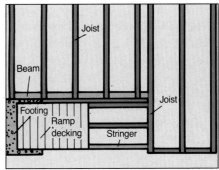

This plan drawing of a ramp shows the relationship of ramp to landing at the deck level.

CUTTING A STRINGER

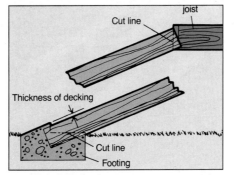

Hold the stringer against the joist and the footing and mark it for cutting.

SPLICING A STRINGER

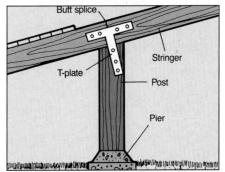

Splice stringers with a butt joint placed over a post and joined with metal T-plates.

STEP 2
CUTTING THE STRINGERS

Cut stringers from 2 × 12s. If you need to splice pieces, make butt joints reinforced with metal plates. Joints must rest on 4 × 4 posts on footings.

STEP 3
MAKING THE RAMP FOOTING

Precast ramp footings are sometimes available. Or, build a wood form for concrete and insert connector hardware.

STEP 4
ATTACHING STRINGERS

Bolt the bottom end of the stringers to the connector hardware embedded in the footing. Use joist hangers to join the stringers to the joist at right angles.

STEP 5
INSTALLING THE DECKING

Nail 2 × 4 decking boards to the stringers with galvanized 10-penny nails. Leave ⅛ inch space between the boards, and ¼ inch between the first board and footing.

RAILINGS FOR STAIRS AND RAMPS

All stairs and ramps up to 6 feet wide should have railings. Stairs of one or two steps, or very wide stairs and ramps, may not need railings. Check local codes.

STEP 1
CUTTING RAILING POSTS

Cut 4 × 4 posts and bolt them vertically to the stringers at the top and bottom, no more than 5 feet apart.

STEP 2
CUTTING THE POST TOPS

Run a chalk line across the posts parallel to the stringers and mark cut lines so that the top of the cap board will be at least 30 inches above the tread. Cut off the post tops with a circular saw.

STEP 3
INSTALLING CAP BOARDS AND FILL-IN

Nail 2 × 4 or 2 × 6 cap boards to the post tops (see page 106). For fill-in install additional boards parallel to the stringers or perpendicular to the treads as desired.

A PRECAST RAMP FOOTING

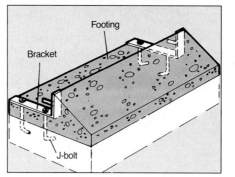

Use a precast concrete footing for the ramp, if available, with hardware already installed.

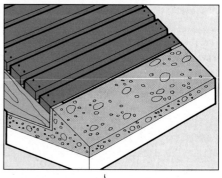

2. Install top end of stringers in metal joist hangers; you may have to notch stringer end.

INSTALLING STRINGERS

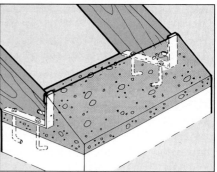

1. Join stringers to the footing connectors. Leave room for decking top to meet footing flush.

LAYING THE DECKING

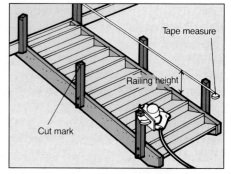

Nail the decking to the stringers, leaving a ¼-inch gap between pieces and at the footing.

BUILDING RAILINGS FOR STAIRS AND RAMPS

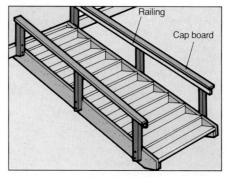

1. Bolt 4 × 4 posts to the stringers and to the joist. Mark railing location at top edges.

3. Nail or screw inside horizontal railings and cap boards in place on posts.

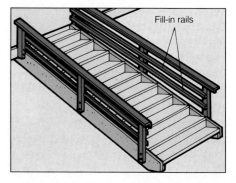

2. Make sure cut marks are in line; use a circular saw to cut post tops.

4. Install additional horizontal or vertical fill-in boards as desired.

Good deck design incorporates natural features such as existing trees whenever possible. Extensive construction such as this requires careful planning and plenty of help, perhaps even a professional contractor.

(Right) Shadows on the rear wall reveal the louvered construction of an overhead covering that is supported by posts on one side and a balcony on the other.

(Below) The spa and table area on this ground-level deck are masked from one direction by latticework fencing.

(Opposite) Weathered wood and carefully spaced sets of triple verticals are the fundamental design elements in the railings and screens of this extensive multilevel deck.

A bench-railing borders the upper level of this poolside deck. The lower level, three steps down, is flush with the paving around the pool edge.

Tucked away for privacy, this spa corner features a railing that is easy to construct. The post top detail can be made of two blocks, or of short pieces nailed around the sides. At the opposite end of the deck, broad steps flanked by planters lead to the latticework entrance.

The boxlike construction of planters, walls, and deck harmonizes well with this shingled house.

(Above) Railing posts and balusters are attached to the skirt and cap joists of the deck. Latticework below masks the foundation structure but allows plenty of air circulation to avoid mustiness and damp rot.

(Right) This two-story deck is elevated enough for the space below to be used for storage cf lawn furniture and pool accessories.

(Below) The deck area and its access walk are supported by piers sunk into the water, but seem to float just above the surface.

(Opposite) The use of redwood and matched construction in the porch, deck, steps, and furniture creates a striking effect.

(Right) Cantilevered construction supports a deck that overlooks the pool from the second-story level.

(Below) A screened-in deck area is protected by a full roof with skylight panels over the doors.

(Opposite) Easy-to-make triangle platforms laid on the ground lead to a garden picnic deck.

A railing of elegant simplicity borders this raised deck, connected by stairs to decking around an unusual trapezoidal pool. The railing posts are set back from the corners, a visually interesting detail. Deck access on the other side of the house is by stairs from ground level.

(Below) Low walls of tongue-and-groove lumber and an angled corner gate provide a clean, modern-looking enclosure for this decked pool area.

(Opposite) Decking can emphasize the outline of an unusual pool, or it can complement a traditional pool shape.

(Right) The broad cap board on this wood railing is a comfortable place to rest one's arms while enjoying the view.

(Below) The parallel lines of the decking and the railing cap match those of the house siding for an integrated appearance.

This ocean-view deck provides a level area for furniture. The pipe-and-standard railing offers safety without obstructing the view.

The open construction and stainless steel railing of this deck complement the contemporary design of the house. Railing posts were bolted to deck and stair members through plates welded at their bottom ends. Then steel cables with turnbuckles to draw them taut were added as fill-in. A shaded dining area on the deck is accessible through a cutaway corner entrance to the living room.

Substantial concrete piers support a railing made of polished steel pipe. The piers were poured after the railing was in position. The clean, simple line of the railing sets off the ground-level deck area without interfering with the view. The flooring is laid parallel to the long dimension of the pool and is fitted to its free-form shape.

The main entrance of this home is enhanced by low decks and walkway platforms that lead to the driveway. The design incorporates an existing tree to provide a pleasant spot for a bench. Unobtrusive deck-level fixtures light the walkway at night.

The steps to the interior floor repeat this deck's pentagon shape, which is also emphasized by the broad perimeter bench. Steps are illuminated by lights built into flanking box planters.

One deck supports another for two viewing levels over steeply sloping terrain. Access to the upper deck is through sliding glass doors on the top floor of the house.

The materials and design of this deck integrate the house with its woodland site. Wood facing over retaining walls harmonizes with plantings and the natural growth beyond. The outdoors is visually joined with the indoors by the glass walls and roof of a conservatory.

An impressive wide stairway, made of treads on notched stringers, leads to a deck that surrounds the house. The broad area overlooking the pool includes railing benches and built-in trees. A zigzag railing with angled posts and mitered cap joints is an energetic design element. Solid fill-in between deck and ground level conceals the deck supports and the house foundation.

(Below) The outer section of this overhead covering is made of close-spaced stringers on edge, fastened on top of their joists. The inner section is made of more widely spaced stringers, laid flat and fastened to the underside of the joists.

(Opposite) This roof uses lathing and 1× lumber to achieve both lightness and strength. Double-board beams and rafters attach to the main posts. Intermediate rafters attach to short posts hanging from the beam. The covering of spaced lath provides an interesting pattern of shade.

Redwood is an excellent choice to help blend natural features with man-made materials in this quiet corner rock garden.

9 WOOD DECK SCREENS

If the people using your deck are bothered by wind, sun, rain, insects, or a lack of privacy or security, some kind of screen may solve the problem.

Partial screens, carefully placed, can eliminate undesirable wind, rain, and sun, and in some cases provide for satisfactory privacy. Insects, on the other hand, cannot be kept out unless you enclose the deck within a total screen structure. Any degree of security usually requires a substantial wall of masonry, wood, or metal fencing. It is also possible to provide protection from wind and prying eyes by planting trees and bushes.

Masonry, metal, and glass structures, as well as landscaping and planting, are outside the subject area of this book. Overhead coverings for decks are discussed in Chapter 10.

In this chapter, we discuss two types of wood screens for decks. The first is a partial wood screen that is either integral with the deck structure itself or built close by. The purpose of this screen is to deflect or modify undesirable wind currents, to provide partial privacy, and perhaps create a little shade. The basic design is similar to that described earlier, with 4 × 4 posts for main support, and smaller-size lumber as fill-in.

The second type is a total screening-in of the deck with a roof covering and framework attached to the deck. This structure will eliminate insects from the deck area, as well as provide shade and protection from rain.

A SOLID WOOD DECK SCREEN

A wood deck screen creates visual privacy, controls prevailing breezes, provides some acoustical privacy, and enhances the enclosed atmosphere of the deck.

A DECK ENCLOSED WITH MESH SCREENS

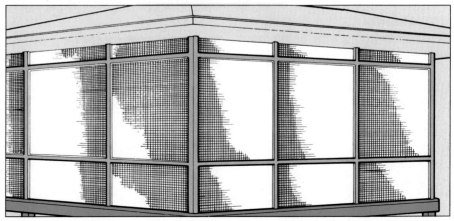

The primary purpose of completely enclosing a deck with roof and screens is to eliminate insect pests. Protection from rain is also provided.

BUILDING A PARTIAL WOOD SCREEN

A wood screen on one or more sides of your deck can give privacy or block wind and noise. If you build a screen at the same time as the deck, you can use the deck posts to support it. If you want to add a screen later, you can set the supports in the ground at any convenient location, or attach them to the deck joists.

STEP 1
BUILDING THE FRAMEWORK

A screen can be built as an integral part of the deck by extending the 4 × 4 deck posts as supports; beams will be attached to the sides of these posts (see page 102). If the screen is built apart from the deck, place the 4 × 4s on concrete footings (see pages 84–85). Install horizontal members as described on page 105.

STEP 2
FILLING IN THE FRAMEWORK

For maximum protection, build a solid screen by nailing tongue-and-groove boards to one side of the framework. To let in some breeze but retain privacy, use an alternating pattern of 1× boards. For a more open effect, make a latticework fill-in, either at right angles or 45-degree angles to the framework.

MAKING A WIND BAFFLE

To create a more effective wind baffle, add an angled extension to the top of a solid screen (see page 24).

STEP 1
INSTALLING EXTENSIONS

Cut a notch in one side of the top of each 4 × 4 support post. Cut 2 × 4s to fit these notches. Drill holes for two bolts through both pieces and bolt them together.

STEP 2
ADDING EXTENSION FILL-IN

Nail 2 × 4s across the tops of the baffle frame extensions. Continue the fill-in from the vertical screen up across the extension. Where the boards meet between vertical frame and extension, make a mitered joint.

SETTING UP A SCREEN FRAMEWORK

A screen attached to the deck itself can best be supported by extending the deck posts.

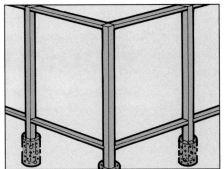

Framework for a free-standing screen can be supported by 4 × 4 posts in concrete footings.

A SOLID WOOD FILL-IN

A solid wood screen is easily made by nailing tongue-and-groove boards to the framework shown above. Toenail the boards in place as shown at right.

TYPES OF OPEN WOOD FILL-IN

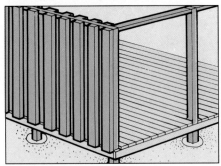

Nail strips of 1x lumber vertically to the framework shown at the top of the page.

Nail strips of lath diagonally in a criss-cross pattern to the framework.

MAKING A WIND BAFFLE

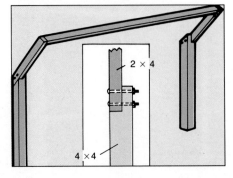

1. Bolt a framework extension made of 2 × 4s to the 4 × 4 posts at an angle.

2. Nail tongue-and-groove boards across the posts and the extension framework.

ENCLOSING A DECK WITH SCREENING

If you plan from the beginning to build a screened-in deck, you can use the deck posts to support the screens and the overhead cover (see Chapter 10). To keep out insects, lay solid decking, of 2 × 4s or 2 × 6s tightly together, or tongue-and-groove flooring. If you screen in the deck later, the overhead support can be attached to the joists as shown at right, and solid flooring laid over the old.

STEP 1
MAKING THE OVERHEAD SUPPORT

The screens and the roof cover can be supported either by extended 4 × 4 deck posts or by 4 × 4s attached to the deck joists as shown at right.

STEP 2
BUILDING THE COVER

You can build a solid rainproof roof (as described in Chapter 10) or use screens for the overhead cover, supported by a light framework.

STEP 3
INSTALLING SCREENS

If possible, plan your screen supports to accommodate commercial, standard size wood or metal frames. Install the screening in these frames using a spline tool and holding strip. If commercial sizes don't fit your deck, make custom screens.

MAKING CUSTOM SCREENS
STEP 1
MAKING THE FRAMES

Cut four pieces of 1 × 2 lumber to fit your framework openings, then miter the corners. Glue the frame pieces together with exterior waterproof glue, and hammer corrugated fasteners across the mitered joints.

STEP 2
INSTALLING THE SCREENING

Lay a roll of fiberglass, nylon, or metal screening across the frame. Staple and stretch the screening, alternating from one side to the other, and working out from the center. Use copper-coated staples to avoid rust or corrosion. Nail half-round molding over the staples.

ATTACHING POST TO DECK

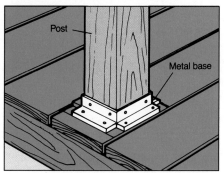

Posts to support screen framework can be attached to the decking with a metal plate.

POST BETWEEN JOISTS

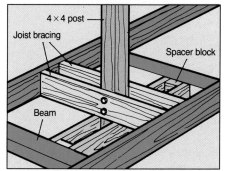

A post can be installed anywhere between joists as long as sufficient support is provided.

A DESIGN FOR AN OVERHEAD SCREEN COVER

A lightweight wood framework can support screens to totally enclose the deck, as shown above, or other types of overhead cover, as described in the next chapter.

MAKING SCREEN FRAMES

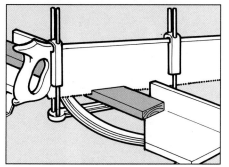

1. Use a miter box to cut mitered corners in the 1 × 2 lumber that forms the screen frames.

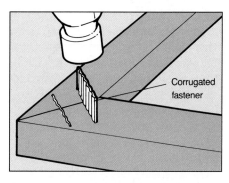

2. Drive one or two corrugated fasteners across the mitered corners to secure them.

INSTALLING SCREENING

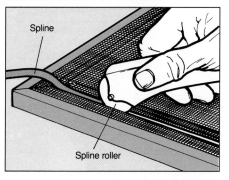

Install screening in commercial frames with a holding strip wedged in place with a spline tool.

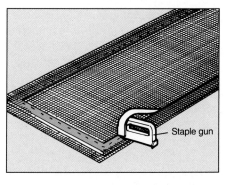

Install screening on custom-made frames with a staple gun; stretch screening taut.

STEP 3
SECURING SCREENS TO FRAMEWORK

To install the screens permanently, toenail them with 8-penny nails 18 inches apart. To install the screens temporarily—so that they can easily be taken down and stored away—first nail a molding of 2 × 2s all around the inside of the framework. Then screw turnbuttons at the top and sides to hold the screens in place.

STEP 4
MAKING A DOOR FRAME

If you want a door for a screened-in deck, purchase a prebuilt screen door with hardware, including hinges. Then build a frame to fit it. Make the frame absolutely vertical and square so the door will hang and swing properly.

STEP 5
HANGING THE DOOR

Decide whether you want the door to swing out of or into the area before you begin. First attach hinges to the door 10 to 12 inches from the bottom and the top. Then hold the door in the frame with 10-penny nails or slim wedges of wood as spacers at the top and on the hinge side. Mark the frame through the hinge screw holes. Remove the door to drill pilot holes, then replace it, with the spacers in position, and screw the hinges to the frame. Take the spacers out and check the door motion. File or plane down any edge that binds.

STEP 6
INSTALLING THE DOORSTOP

Wedge the screen door in closed position and mark lines on the frame all around the top and sides of the door. Cut pieces of doorstop molding (a standard item at lumberyards) to fit the three sides of the doorframe and miter them at the top corners. Nail the molding along the marked lines with finishing nails every 10 to 12 inches.

STEP 7
INSTALLING A CATCH

Use the templates that come with the door catch to mark the position of holes to be drilled. Place the catch about 36 inches above the deck level. The strike plate is screwed to the molding.

INSTALLING PERMANENT SCREENS

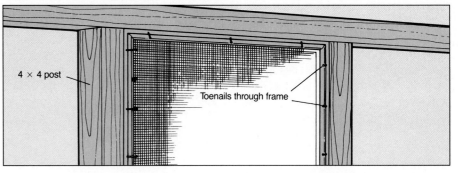

For permanent screen installation, set the frames in position and toenail them to the posts that support the overhead cover.

INSTALLING REMOVABLE SCREENS

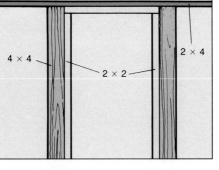

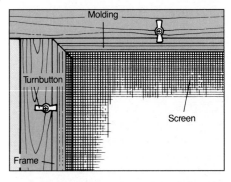

1. Nail 2 × 2 molding inside the support posts just deep enough to hold the screens flush with the posts.

2. Install turn buttons on the posts and along the top to hold the screen firmly against the molding.

INSTALLING A SCREEN DOOR

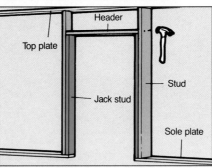

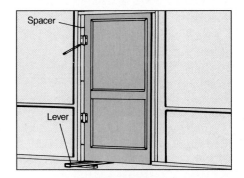

1. Install studs, jack studs, and header within the frame to fit a prehung door.

2. Set the door between the jack studs, and while levering up the bottom, install hinges.

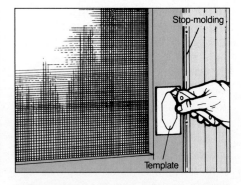

3. While holding the door closed, mark the jack studs and header for the stop molding.

4. Cut a hole in the door using the template provided; install door catch and strike plate.

10 OVERHEAD COVER FOR DECKS

Overhead cover makes a deck more of an outdoor room. The roof structure defines the space but still allows a feeling of openness. This chapter describes how to build wood deck coverings for a variety of purposes. Although the design and structural ideas shown are basic, they can be elaborated to create coverings to fill your own needs.

The basic overhead framework shown on this page can be used simply to define the deck area. With the addition of fill-in, such as louvers, latticework, or canvas (see pages 150–151), varying degrees of shade can be created for the deck area. By building a trellis across the framework, support can be provided for vines or other growth that will beautify the deck area.

The framework can serve as a support structure for insectproof screens to enclose the entire deck (see Chapter 9). In regions where wind and rain are troublesome, the addition of a permanent, rainproof roof will make it possible to use the deck for more months out of the year.

When combined with a wall or fence, a roof structure increases privacy. Separate elements, such as carport and house or garden and deck can be linked with an overhead cover.

Preliminary planning as well as design principles and site preparation are discussed in chapters 1 through 4. Special structural requirements for wood coverings are given in the chart on page 151. Construction techniques are also discussed in Chapter 5.

A DESIGN FOR A BASIC DECK COVER

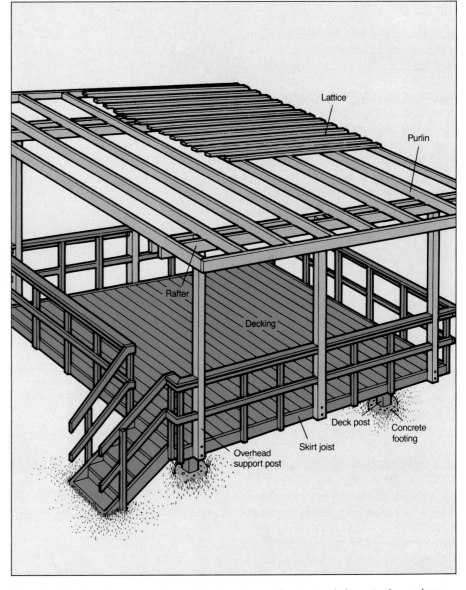

A standard framework to support a wood deck cover uses the structural elements shown above.

BUILDING AN OVERHEAD WOOD STRUCTURE

The deck covering shown here is integrated with the basic deck structure described in Chapter 5. The sizes of dimension lumber to be used for various structures are given in the chart opposite. The support posts may be secured as shown here or to the deck joists, as shown on page 105. These posts may be integrated with the deck railing (see Chapter 7).

STEP 1
SETTING UP THE POSTS

The posts for the overhead structure may be the same ones that support the deck. You may extend all the exterior deck posts or only widely spaced ones, as long as they meet support requirements. If your deck sits on the ground, without posts, or you are adding a roof at a later time, attach the support posts to the deck with metal bases.

STEP 2
INSTALLING THE BEAMS

In this design, pairs of 2 × 10s bolted to the posts form the main supporting beams. About 24 inches of overhang has been used at both ends. With a helper, first tack-nail the beams in place and then make sure they are properly aligned before fastening them permanently. The bottom of the beam should be at least 84 inches above the level of the deck.

STEP 3
SETTING THE PURLINS

The next level of the structure, called the purlins, consists of 2 × 6s set on edge at right angles to the beams and toenailed in place. In this design the purlins are 24 inches on center. If desired, 2 × 6 fascia boards can be nailed across the ends of the purlins, to provide additional stability.

STEP 4
INSTALLING FILL-IN

Latticework fill-in can be made from 2 × 2 strips of wood placed at right angles to or diagonally across the purlins. A second layer of 2 × 2s can be nailed to the first layer from underneath. A denser fill-in can be made from 1 × 4s nailed close together across the purlins; this creates a louvered cover.

EXTENDED DECK POSTS

The posts that support the deck can be extended to support the overhead framework.

SETTING POSTS ON THE DECKING

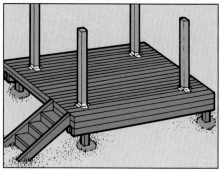

Posts to support overhead framing can be set anywhere on the decking, using metal foot plates.

ATTACHING BEAMS TO POSTS

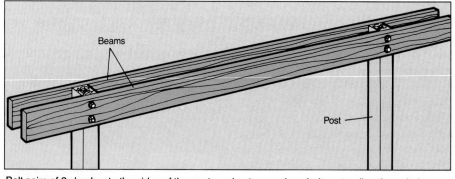

Bolt pairs of 2x lumber to the sides of the posts, using two carriage bolts extending through the post. Beams may be level or slanted as desired.

SETTING UP PURLINS AND FASCIA BOARDS

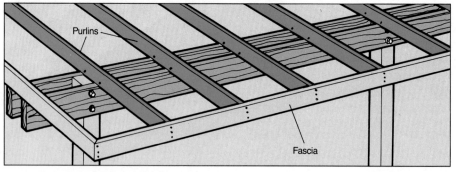

Set purlins at right angles to the beams and toenail them in place. Nail fascia boards across the ends of the purlins for stability.

TYPES OF WOOD OVERHEAD FILL- IN

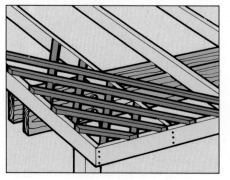

Pieces of 2 × 2 lumber can be nailed diagonally across purlins, or in a criss-cross pattern.

Nail 1 × 4s with beveled edges at right angles to the purlins to make a louvered cover.

ADDITIONAL TYPES OF FILL-IN

The basic overhead structure described on the previous pages can support many different kinds of covering materials, including wood, plastic, and canvas.

LATH FILL-IN

Lathing is thin, narrow strips of flexible, lightweight wood. To make a deck covering, nail laths to the purlins (see Step 3, page 150) with ½-inch spacing. This lets sun and rain filter through the cracks. This design can save tax dollars, since some communities do not categorize lath structures as permanent buildings and therefore impose no tax on them. If you use cedar or redwood lath, let the structure weather naturally. Otherwise, apply a coat of weather-resistant latex stain or paint.

FIBERGLASS PANELS

Use the structure described on pages 149–150, but set the purlins 24 inches on center to accommodate the standard 26-inch fiberglass panels, which will overlap one corrugation on each side. Also, give the purlins a good pitch, that is, let the roof rise about 3 inches for every 12 inches of span. This provides adequate drainage of rain and snow. To prevent sagging, add cross bracing every 5 feet between the purlins. Use aluminum nails and neoprene washers to attach the panels to the purlins. Predrill the nail holes.

CANVAS COVERING

In dry climates a canvas overhead cover will last a long time and provide shade and rain protection at a relatively low cost. The easiest installation method is to tie the stretched fabric to a wood frame or to a pipe frame, as shown at right. The canvas can be hemmed at an awning shop, or you can sew up to No. 10 weight canvas yourself, using a No. 13 sailmaker's needle and Dacron thread. The awning shop can also put in grommets, or you can do it yourself, using a grommet die and die block. A tied-on canvas cover requires grommets placed every 8 inches and at each corner.

Use ¼-inch diameter cord or rope to lash the canvas to a framework.

ROOF STRUCTURAL REQUIREMENTS
For roof to be supported by house on one or more sides, without overhang.

ROOF AREA	RAFTERS Spacing	RAFTERS Size	BEAMS Number	BEAMS Size	POSTS* Number	POSTS* Spacing
8' × 16'	12" o.c.	8'2" × 4"	2	8'2" × 8"	3	8' o.c.
	16" o.c.	8'2" × 4"	2	8'4" × 6"	Same	
	24" o.c.	8'2" × 6"	1	16'2" × 14"	2	16' o.c.
8' × 24'	Same		2	12'2" × 10"	4	8' o.c.
			2	12'4" × 6"	Same	
			3	8'2" × 8"	5	6' o.c.
10' × 16'	16" o.c.	10'2" × 6"	2	8'2" × 8"	3	8' o.c.
	24" o.c.	10'2" × 6"	2	8'4" × 6"	Same	
10' × 24'	Same		2	12'2" × 12"	3	12' o.c.
			2	12'4" × 8"	Same	
12' × 16'	12" o.c.	12'2" × 6"	2	8'2" × 10"	3	8' o.c.
	16" o.c.	12'2" × 6"	2	8'4" × 6"	Same	
	24" o.c.	12'2" × 8"	1	16'4" × 12"	2	16' o.c.
12' × 24'	Same		2	12'2" × 12"	3	12' o.c.
			2	12'4" × 8"	4	8' o.c.
16' × 16'	16" o.c.	16'2" × 8"	2	8'2" × 10"	3	8' o.c.
	24" o.c.	16'2" × 10"	1	16'4" × 14"	2	16' o.c.
16' × 24'	Same		3	8'2" × 10"	4	8' o.c.
			3	8'4" × 8"	Same	
			2	12'2" × 14"	3	12' o.c.

*Use 4 × 4 posts for spacing up to 5 feet, 4 × 6 posts for spacing from 6 to 8 feet, and 6 × 6 posts for spacing over 8 feet.

ADDITIONAL TYPES OF OVERHEAD COVER

Strips of lath can be nailed to the purlins to make as dense or as open a cover as desired.

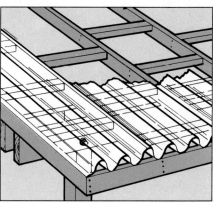

Corrugated fiberglass panels make a long-lasting lightweight overhead cover. Give the roof a good pitch for adequate drainage.

A DESIGN FOR CANVAS DECK COVERING

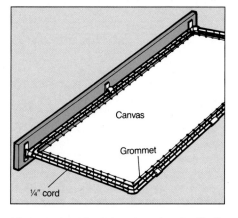

A framework made of pipe or wood can be filled in with stretched canvas to provide low-cost shade and protection from rain.

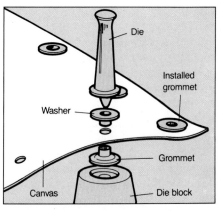

Grommets for lashing the canvas to the frame can be installed with die, dieblock, and hammer.

BUILDING A RETRACTABLE CANVAS DECK COVER

If your deck needs only occasional protection from sun and rain, consider this adjustable awning designed by the California Redwood Association. The heavyweight canvas awning extends and retracts by a rope and pulley system. It can be installed on the overhead framework described in this chapter, provided the purlins are pitched to give adequate runoff. Use canvas in the normal 76-inch width, or sew narrower panels together to fit.

STEP 1
SEWING DOWEL TUNNELS
Sew folds across the canvas, using 3½ inches of material, to make dowel tunnels; leave 14 inches between seams. Double-stitch each seam.

STEP 2
INSTALLING THE DOWELS
Cut lengths of ¾-inch doweling to fit the width of your canvas strip, and insert them in the tunnels.

STEP 3
INSTALLING SUPPORT PIPES
Use three ½-inch galvanized metal pipes to support each awning strip. The pipes run at right angles to the roof slope. Slip 1½-inch metal rings over the pipes, enough to support each dowel; put half the rings in each side of the center support. Use screw hooks at the ends and in the center of each pipe to secure it to the purlins.

STEP 4
CONNECTING DOWELS TO PIPES
Put three screw eyes through the canvas tunnel into each dowel; match the spacing of the pipe supports. Use tent wall snaps to connect each screw eye to a metal ring on the pipe.

STEP 5
INSTALLING THE CONTROL ROPE
Connect the control rope to the center ring at both ends of the awning, so that the halves move in opposite directions when the rope is pulled, opening and closing to and from the center.

A DESIGN FOR A RETRACTING CANVAS DECK COVER

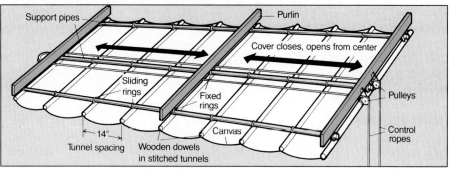

Sheets of canvas, sewn to dowels that are hung from pipes, open and close in two sections, controlled by ropes running on pulleys.

INSTALLING DOWELS IN TUNNELS

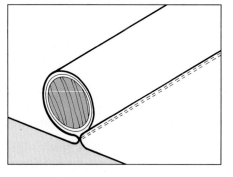 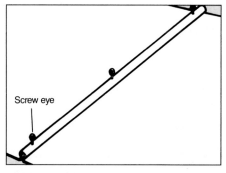

Insert ¾-inch dowels into tunnels sewn in canvas with double seams.

Three screw eyes are installed through the canvas into the dowel tops, opposite the seam.

HARDWARE TO SUPPORT THE DOWELS

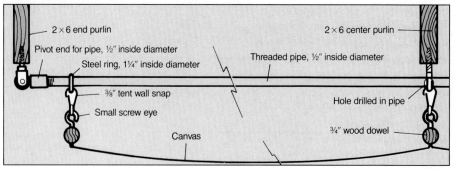

The screw eyes connect to tent wall snaps that hang from steel rings that slide along the pipes.

DIAGRAM OF ROPE INSTALLATION

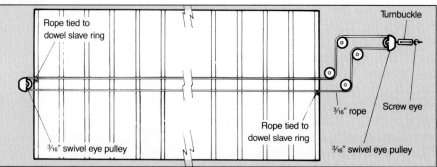

A continuous run of rope is tied only to the rings at the outside ends of the canvas sheets on opposite sides, so that the two canvas sections move in opposite directions.

VINES SUITABLE FOR ROOF TRELLIS COVER

Name	Northern-most Survival Zone	Requirements	Description
Virginia Creeper *Parthenocissus quinquefolia*	Zone 3	Full sun to total shade, good soil and fertilizer.	Height to 30 ft., deciduous, medium green leaves, bluish-black fruit, red fall color. Grows rapidly, needs pruning, drapes over walls, trellises or as ground cover.
Boston Ivy *Parthencissus Tricuspidata*	Zone 4	Good garden soil, half to heavy shade. Young plants need regular watering.	Height to 60 ft., shiny 3-lobed leaves with small, blue berries (attracts birds). Scarlet in fall, deciduous, rapid growth. Clings to stone.
Wisteria *W. Floribunda*	Zone 4	Full sun to partial shade, roots planted deep, garden soil. Water young plants regularly. Stake, prune each year.	Deciduous, fragrant, pendulous flowers (white, lavender or purple) profuse in early summer. May take several years before first bloom.
Ivy *Hedra*	Zone 5	Light to heavy shade, good garden soil. Prune yearly.	Evergreen in milder climates, dense, shiny leaves. Grows vigorously once established.
Anemone Clematis *Clematis Montana*	Zone 6	Rich, slightly alkaline soil. Cool, moist location. Water to establish and during drought. Mulch base to keep roots cool.	Deciduous, height to 20 ft. Leaves and flowers like full sun, base like shade. Grows well under right conditions, will grow on trees, hedges, posts, walls or arbors. Prune for shaping after flowering.
Common Jasmine *Jasminum Officinale*	Zone 7	Full sun to light shade, frequent light watering, good garden soil.	Height to 30 ft., semi-evergreen (warm climate). Fragrant white flowers. Grows easily in southern areas.
Bougainvillea	Zone 10	Full sun, southern exposure, rich loamy soil. Water frequently while growing.	Height to 20 ft. Evergreen in warm climate. Bracts around small flowers give yellow, purple, magenta color in spring and early autumn. Can be *espaliered* (trained) against wall if desired.
Silver Lace Vine *Polygonum Aubertii*	Any	*Annual*, soak seeds to encourage germination. Tolerates dry soil.	Any height, rapid growth which may choke out other plantings. Long flowering period. Does well in adverse urban conditions.

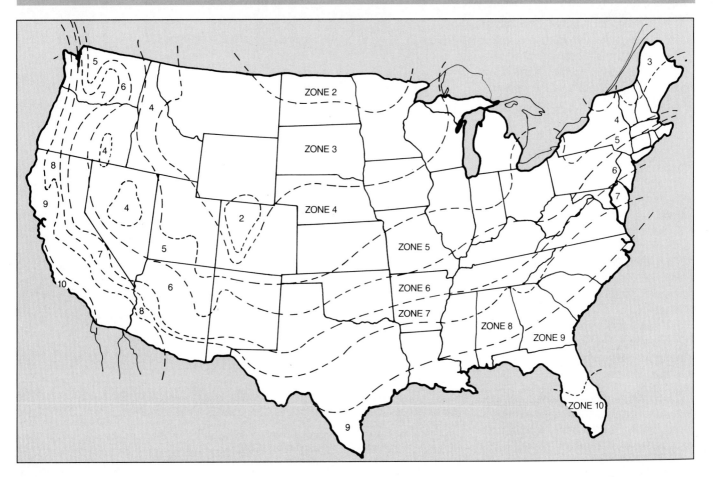

11 OUTDOOR LIGHTING

Exterior lighting, when placed wisely around a deck, can enhance and extend the usefulness of exterior space. Accent lighting creates a mood and even adds to the apparent size of an outdoor deck. Whether you want to light walkways and paths for safety, spotlight an important area or feature, or provide overall illumination for evening entertainment, follow these basic rules:

1. Provide enough light for the job at hand, but do not over-light. Too much light can ruin the atmosphere of an outside space; too much light often causes surface glare. Use several small lights, carefully placed, rather than one or two powerful ones.

2. Arrange the lighting so that the illumination is seen but not the source. Any bare spotlight is unsightly. Use indirect lighting, which casts a uniform light level without emphasizing its source.

3. Backlighting at night creates a visual effect that is seldom possible during the day. It can transform a commonplace location by means of dramatic shadows and decorative effects.

4. Keep the distance between lights to a minimum. The more spread out the lighting is, the more expensive the installation will be.

Exterior lighting falls into two categories: functional and decorative. Functional lighting is necessary illumination for safe use of outdoor stairs, walk-

LIGHTING FOR A DECK AND SURROUNDING AREA

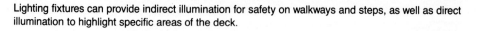

Lighting fixtures can provide indirect illumination for safety on walkways and steps, as well as direct illumination to highlight specific areas of the deck.

ways, and grills. Take care of functional lighting first. Decorative lighting can be added as you wish to enhance the atmosphere of your deck.

EXTERIOR ELECTRICAL POWER

Indoor and outdoor electrical circuits are identical, but the materials used for exterior power distribution are different. All exterior receptacles must be waterproof, with either snap-closing or screw-on covers. Place exterior power receptacles where you will be using appliances for outdoor entertaining or where an outdoor lighting source will be located. For safety, appliance receptacles must not be on the same circuit as the lighting. You can buy exterior lighting fixtures with built-in receptacles. If at all possible, all exterior power circuits should be controlled from inside the house.

Most electrical codes require that you install Ground Fault Circuit Interrupters (GFCIs) on all outdoor circuits. These safety devices prevent short circuits and electrical shock. They are relatively expensive; therefore, their placement should be carefully planned. If you have a master control unit or an automatic time switch to power outdoor lighting, you must install an override device at a remote location. Most control units have this provision incorporated in their design. Keep lighting circuits separate from other exterior power circuits.

EXTERIOR CIRCUIT VOLTAGE

There are two basic types of exterior lighting available: standard voltage (120 volts) and low voltage (12 volts). Before you install any system, find out from the building inspector's office what is acceptable. Although the National Electric Code applies in most areas, there may be local amendments. A low-voltage system is useful for a small deck or garden area; the standard 120-volt system is recommended for large areas.

Many different lighting fixtures are available. Some are intended only for in-ground application; others are only used for wall mounting. Only buy fixtures designed specifically for outdoor use.

DRILLING THROUGH SIDING

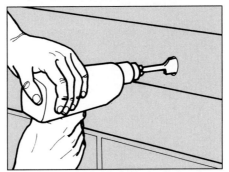

Bore a hole through the siding and the header or joist with a ⅞-inch spade bit.

INSTALLING INTERIOR BOX

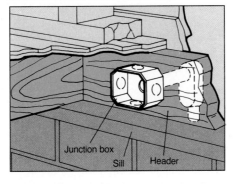

On the inside, the junction box will be placed over the hole in the header.

INSTALLING FITTINGS

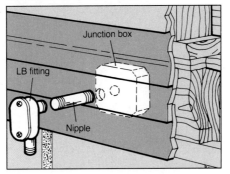

1. On the outside, the LB fitting is attached to the nipple, which extends through the hole.

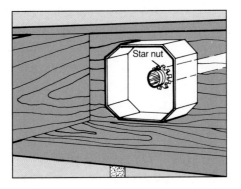

2. The junction box is secured to the inside end of the nipple with a star nut.

PLANNING OUTDOOR CIRCUITS

Using the plan of your property (see Chapter 3), locate your electrical service panel. This will make clear the path that the power will follow from the interior to the exterior of the house. Mark the locations of lighting fixtures, receptacles, and exterior switches according to your design. Use three-way switches that will give you control from inside the house. If you are planning installations in both the front and back of the house, it is a good idea to use separate circuits.

Plan all fixture and receptacle locations so that installation and maintenance are easy. Try to keep the total distance between fixtures to a minimum. By laying out a plan for all circuits, you can estimate quantities of materials, fixtures, and tools you'll need to do the job.

UNDERGROUND ELECTRICAL MATERIALS

Before running a cable from inside the house to the outside, you must decide on the type of wire to be used and how the circuits will be built. Most codes require that all outdoor wiring be placed in rigid conduit from the point where it leaves the house to the point where it goes underground. Check your local code to determine the specific requirements. UF cable, a plastic-sheathed cable designed to be buried in the ground, can be used for most underground wiring. It is sold in two- or three-wire configuration plus a ground wire. You may be able to use conduit underground with TW wire, which has a moisture-resistant covering. Rigid conduit comes in three types: thin-wall plastic, thin-wall metal (EMT), and thick-wall metal. When used for underground runs, all types of conduit must be placed at least 12 inches deep.

INSTALLATION PROCEDURES

If you are not familiar with electrical wiring procedures or circuitry, have a licensed electrician connect the wiring; some local codes require this in any case. But you can save on labor costs by doing some installation work—explained here—ahead of time.

CONNECTING INTERIOR-EXTERIOR CIRCUITS

You can connect interior wiring to an exterior conduit through a frame wall or through the foundation wall. For a connection through a foundation, the junction boxes (to which the conduit will be attached) must be placed over an opening on the inside of the wall, so that the nipple extends through the wall into the box. Drill the hole at a point where you know you will not interfere with other utilities and where you will have easy outdoor access.

WORKING THROUGH WOOD SIDING
STEP 1
DRILLING THE HOLES

Place the LB fitting where you plan to drill and check that the fitting will not overlap a siding joint. Drill a ¼-inch test hole to double-check measurements. Then use a ⅞-inch spade bit to bore a hole through the joist.

STEP 2
INSTALLING THE HARDWARE

Mount the junction box on the interior over the hole. Use a nipple that reaches through the wall to the box, and screw the nipple to an LB fitting. Put the nipple in the hole to test its fit. Bend the conduit so that it runs from the fitting into the trench. Remove the nipple and LB fitting, connect them to the conduit, and put the nipple back into the hole. Strap the conduit to the outside foundation and caulk all around the nipple. Inside, at the junction box, attach the nipple using a star nut and then screw a plastic bushing onto the nut.

WORKING THROUGH CINDERBLOCK
STEP 1
DRILLING THE HOLES

Use a ⅞-inch star drill to make an outside hole through the second course down from the siding; the blocks should be hollow at this point. Pound the hole through. For a clear, round hole, rotate the drill ⅛ turn after each hammer tap.

To make the inside hole for a box, place the box against the block and outline its shape with tape. Drill 6 to 8 holes into the center of the block, using

DRILLING THROUGH MASONRY

1. From the outside, make a hole through the block with a ⅞-inch star drill.

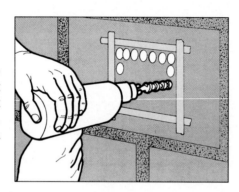

2. On the inside of the block, drill and hammer out a hole to fit the junction box.

INSTALLING THE JUNCTION BOX

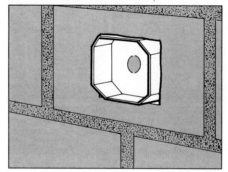

1. On the inside, slip the junction box into the hole in the masonry block.

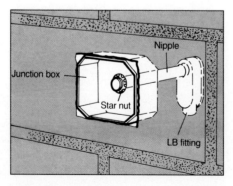

2. Place the nipple through the hole, and secure it inside the box with a star nut.

a ½-inch masonry bit in a ⅜-inch drill. Use a ball-peen hammer and a cold chisel to knock away any material left between the drilled holes. Then chip out the edges to hold the box.

If the cinderblock is stuccoed over so that you cannot find the seams, make a test hole with a star drill. When your test probe finds the hollow center (an area where the drill meets no resistance) insert a stick into the hole and tap around to find each side of the hollow. Make a hole to hold the box as described above.

STEP 2
INSTALLING THE HARDWARE

First, loosely insert screws into the fixture mounting straps so mortar won't get into the screw holes. Then adjust the box ears so that the edge of the box is about 1/16 inch from the wall. Slide the box into place and mortar it in (use premixed mortar). Spread the mortar with a putty knife so that the edge of the hole is completely filled; this protects the unit from dampness. When the mortar has dried, take out the screws. Connect the LB fitting and nipple as above.

WORKING THROUGH THE SOFFIT
STEP 1
DRILLING THE HOLE

Have a helper hold the assembled parts. Place the outdoor box, corner, elbow, section of conduit, and nipple against the soffit board. Keep the conduit next to the house and place the box between two rows of nails in the soffit. Using the box as a template, mark the soffit for a cable hole and for mounting screw holes. Use a ³/₃₂-inch bit to drill holes for ¾-inch No. 8 screws; use a 1⅛-inch spade bit to drill a hole for the cable.

STEP 2
MOUNTING THE BOX ON THE SOFFIT

After fishing the cable from an indoor circuit and out through the cable hole, fasten on a two-part connector. You may have to enlarge the cable hole with a rasp before you can line up the mounting tabs on the box with the screw holes. Screw the box to the soffit;

then fasten the conduit to the wall and the nipple to the soffit board. Bend the conduit to run it into the trench.

DIGGING A TRENCH

Stake out the trench to keep it as straight as possible. A trench for conduit should be 8 inches wide and at least 12 inches deep.

SETTING UP RECEPTACLES

Where the conduit comes up out of the trench to support a receptacle or light fixture, bring it up through an open cell in a concrete block. Plan to make the wiring connection at least 12 inches off the ground. If the circuit continues, run the conduit back down through the block and along the trench. Fill the block cells with dirt or gravel.

SETTING UP A LAMP POST
STEP 1
CUTTING THE POST

Mark guidelines, 18 inches long and ⅞ inch apart, down one side of the hollow lamp post. Cut out this strip and smooth any sharp edges or burrs with a metal file. If the post sits in the middle of a run, cut another slot on the side facing the continuing run of conduit.

STEP 2
SETTING UP THE POST

Dig a hole that is 2 feet deep and about 8 inches wide. If you are using UF cable you do not need conduit. For any other cable, curve the conduit to rise into position in the center of the hole. It should rise nearly as high as the lock ring on an adjustable post, or nearly to the top of a fixed-length post. Cap the conduit with a plastic bushing and slip the post over the conduit. Check that the post is vertical. Tamp down alternating layers of dirt and gravel around the post, up to the bottom of the trench. When you backfill the trench later, fill the hole completely.

FISHING CABLE THROUGH THE CONDUIT

If you have the necessary skills, you can now run the cable from the interior junction box, through the conduit, into the receptacles and fixtures, using a fishtape as shown at right. Otherwise, it is time to call the electrician.

INSTALLING A SOFFIT BOX

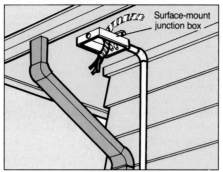

Attach a surface-mount box to the soffit and the conduit to the exterior wall.

SETTING UP RECEPTACLES

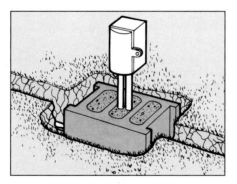

1. At the end of a run, bend the conduit up so that the end is at the desired height.

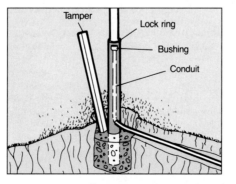

2. Place a concrete block over the end of the conduit; install an exterior-use receptacle.

DIGGING A TRENCH

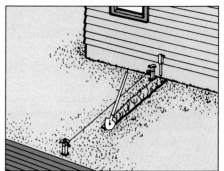

Dig a trench from the LB fitting or from the soffit box at the house to the desired location.

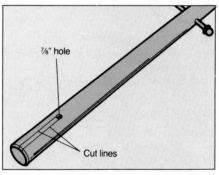

In the middle of a run, bend both pieces of conduit up together, to the desired height.

SETTING UP A LAMP POST

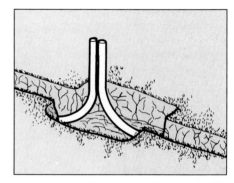

1. Cut a ⅞-inch wide slot at the bottom of the post for the conduit.

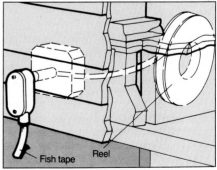

3. Use a fishtape to run electrical cable from inside the house out to post or receptacle.

2. Insert the conduit through the slot and up the post. Bury the post in tamped gravel.

Glossary

Backfill Earth or other material used to fill excavated space around a construction in the ground.

Batter board Piece of lumber mounted horizontal and level on stakes as a support for strings that guide construction.

Beam Heavy piece of lumber that rests horizontally on posts, supporting deck joists.

Blocking Short pieces of joist lumber inserted at right angles between joists to strengthen them.

Board foot Unit of lumber measurement: a quantity of wood 12″ × 12″ × 1″. See linear foot.

Bridging Pieces of lumber fastened in an X pattern between joists to prevent twisting.

Butt joint Two pieces of wood joined by placing their square-cut ends face to face.

Cantilever Construction that extends out beyond its vertical support.

Catch (door catch) The metal piece that protrudes from the hardware on the edge of a door into the strike plate on the door post or jamb.

Chalk line String or cord covered with chalk that is snapped against wood members to make a mark for measurement or cutting.

Clinch To drive overlong nails through boards and bend the points down flat on the other side.

Cleat A small piece of lumber fastened, e.g., to a joist or post, as a support for a ledger or railing.

Curing The slow chemical action that hardens concrete.

Dimension lumber Pieces of wood cut and milled to standard sizes (see nominal dimensions).

Double-head nail Fastener used for temporary wood construction; easily pulled out by the top head.

Dry well Gravel-filled hole used to receive and drain away water runoff.

Elevation Drawing or view of construction showing its vertical members or faces.

Expansion shield Metal connector driven into masonry to hold a fastener, such as a bolt.

Fascia Board(s) facing that covers the ends of decking or purlins for a finished appearance.

Flashing Thin, impervious material, such as an aluminum sheet, placed, e.g., over a ledger to keep water off the wood.

Footing The part of a foundation or support system that is in direct contact with the earth.

Frost line The level below grade (q.v.) beneath which the ground does not freeze.

Galvanizing Coating a metal with a thin layer of zinc to prevent rust. Ungalvanized connectors and fasteners are not suitable for outdoor use.

Grade The ground level. On-grade means at or on the natural ground level.

Header In wood construction, the large structural member set on edge in a wall.

Joist Structural member set parallel across beams to support a floor, roof, or decking.

Joist hanger Metal connector used to join a joist and a beam or ledger so that the tops of both are on the same level.

Lag screw/lag bolt Heavy metal fastener installed with a wrench.

Lath Thin, narrow strips of wood used for filling in screens, trellises, and roofs.

Ledger Horizontal board attached to the side of a house or wall to support a deck or an overhead cover.

Linear foot Unit of lumber measurement consisting of a piece of wood one foot long, of any dimension size. See board foot.

Mitered joint The ends of two pieces of lumber cut at equal angles and joined to make an angled corner. The pieces are cut with a miter box and saw.

Nominal dimensions The identifying dimensions of a piece of lumber (e.g., 2 × 4) which are larger than the actual dimensions (1½″ × 3½″).

On center A point of reference for measuring. "16 inches on center" means 16 inches from the center of one joist, for example, to the center of the next joist.

Penny (abbr. d) Unit of nail measurement; e.g., a 10d nail is 3 inches long.

Plan Drawing or view of a construction from directly overhead.

Plumb (adj.) Vertical, straight, perfectly in line. Plumb bob and line: weight on the end of a string, used to set construction plumb.

Post Heavy piece of lumber set vertically on a footing; supports the beams of a deck.

Purlin Horizontal structural member of a roof or overhead cover; supports lighter-weight fill-in materials.

Riser In stairs, the vertical board supporting the front edge of the tread; sometimes omitted. Rise: the distance between one tread and the next.

Run In stairs, the horizontal distance between one riser (q.v.) and the next.

Running foot See linear foot.

Saddle anchor Metal connector that secures a joist to the top of a beam.

Shim Small piece of wood or other material inserted between construction members, such as a door jamb and frame, to space and position them properly.

Skirt Solid band of wood members around the outside of a structure. Skirt joist: a joist installed across the ends of other joists for additional stability.

Star drill Metal drill with a pointed and grooved end, used with a hammer to make holes in masonry and concrete.

Strike plate Metal piece on the door jamb that receives the door catch.

Stringer In stairs, the diagonal outside board, set on edge, that supports the treads and risers.

Tacknail To nail one structural member to another temporarily with a minimum of nails.

Toenail To nail two pieces of wood together by driving nails at an angle through the edge of one into the other.

Tongue-and-groove Joint in paneling or floorboards, in which a narrow protrusion on one board fits into a narrow groove on the next.

Tread In stairs, the horizontal boards supported by the stringers.